HAVE A SAFE JOURNEY

HAVE A SAFE JOURNEY

The World's First Collection of Short Stories on Road Safety

Foreword by NITIN GADKARI
Special Message by ANAND MAHINDRA

An imprint of Manjul Publishing House Pvt. Ltd.
• 7/32, Ansari Road, Daryaganj, New Delhi 110 002
Website: www.manjulindia.com
Registered Office:
10, Nishat Colony, Bhopal 462 003 - India
Distribution Centres:
Ahmedabad, Bengaluru, Bhopal, Kolkata, Chennai,
Hyderabad, Mumbai, New Delhi, Pune

#HaveASafeJourney is a collaborative initiative of

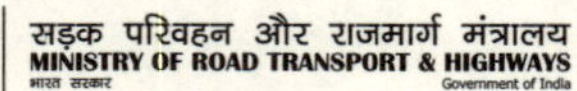

Mahindra
Truck and Bus

ISBN 978-93-81506-98-1

This edition first published in 2017
Second impression 2017

Printed and bound in India by Thomson Press (India) Limited

This is a work of fiction. Names, characters, places and incidents are either the product of the authors' imagination, or are used fictitiously, and any resemblance to any actual person, living or dead, events or locales is entirely coincidental.

CONTENTS

Stories By Our Guest Authors

Stories Chosen From the #HaveASafeJourney Contest

FOREWORD

In the year 2001, I had a close encounter with death when the vehicle I was travelling in rammed head on into another vehicle coming from the opposite direction. So devastating was the impact that I remained bedridden for nearly a year and my recovery from that state can only be described as a miracle. In many ways, this incident was a big turning point in my life. Apart from changing my perspective towards life, it acquainted me with the sheer magnitude of the problem that road accidents pose to a developing nation like ours. Moreover, accident fatalities, being unnatural deaths, often leave behind devastated families and where the victim happens to be the family's breadwinner, the family's ordeal tends to be long-drawn.

Here, I'd like to avoid reinforcing the grim road-accident statistics in India. The media has spoken enough about it. Instead, I want you to just realise that you are not immune to the risk of a road accident, nobody is. As such, a significant onus for preventing road accidents lies upon us, the citizens. That, of course, does not absolve the government of its responsibilities towards the same and the government stands committed to the cause.

Let me quickly acquaint you with the major steps taken by the government in improving road safety.

One of the key decisions of my ministry in addressing this issue has been to extend the total stretch of national highways in the country from a meager 97,000 km to 2,00,000 km in the next five years. India has a total road length of 5.2 million km, but as much as 40 per cent of the traffic that moves on national highways constitutes just 2 per cent of the total road length, thus causing the high accident figures. Doubling the length of national highways will ease traffic and reduce accidents.

Another important step has been conversion of vast stretches of two-lane highways into four-lane highways. Earlier, highways that registered more than 15,000 passenger car units (PCU) per day qualified for conversion to four-lane highways. Now the government has brought down the qualifying criterion to 10,000 PCUs per day. Conversion of two-lane highways into four-lane highways naturally brings down the incidence of road accidents, as there is a bifurcating divider which effectively makes these roads one-way.

The third key initiative has been to involve the public in identifying 'black spots' on the highways. Black spots are the places where maximum accidents occur. After extensive study, the government identified 726 black spots across the country; repair and rectification work is on full swing and hopefully, all these black spots will be addressed in the next few months.

One of the main reasons for the high casualty rate of road accident victims was the huge amount of time wasted in making quality emergency care available to them. To address this, based on a directive from the Honourable Supreme Court, the government has laid out specific guidelines whereby a good Samaritan helping a road victim will not face any harassment from the hospital, police and related authorities. Over a period of time, this step is bound to reduce accident fatalities.

Moreover, the government stands committed to get the Motor Vehicles Amendment Bill passed in Parliament. The bill was introduced by me in August 2016. But since then it has been pending for review with the Parliamentary Standing Committee on Transport, Tourism, and Culture. The focus of the amendment bill, apart from strict norms, is the safety of road users, road accident victims, stricter norms for driving licences and stiffer penalties for law violators.

In addition to all these, my ministry is pushing for intelligent traffic systems which will enable authorities to immediately track, real-time, when there is a traffic violation. Modernising systems with the latest technology is at the top on my ministry's agenda for now.

While these are some of the key steps taken by the government, I firmly believe that NGOs, the corporate sector and citizen groups have an equally important role to play in reducing road-accident fatalities.

In fact, the role of the automobile sector in promoting road safety is very crucial. And here, I wish to laud the efforts of the Mahindra Group and my friend Anand Mahindra for always coming up with innovative initiatives to create awareness about the issue.

I am impressed by the #HaveASafeJourney initiative, which harnesses the power of written stories to educate readers about the gravity of the problem.

Literature has always been a very potent medium in bringing about social changes. I am confident that if our children grow up reading stories about road safety, the issue will be etched deep in their psyche and they will be encouraged to become responsible road users.

Besides, a book on road safety is also likely to subsequently encourage a TV series or a film on the same theme. And hence, over the years, literature and the audiovisual creative media, can be leveraged to raise the road-safety campaign to another level altogether.

Our road-safety campaign needs to become a people's movement. I aspire for the day when every responsible citizen of the country voluntarily takes a pledge to drive safe. This pledge is important, considering the amount of damage one inflicts upon his/her family, as well as other families, by being an irresponsible road user.

Apart from this book, I have asked mass media teaching institutes to come forth and dedicate all their student projects for a given year to road safety.

I am confident that these efforts will increase the participation and involvement of our young citizens in improving road safety.

As of today, we are faced with a stiff target of reducing road accident fatalities by 50 per cent by the year 2020. Though the task is difficult, it is not impossible. In this context, I am very optimistic that initiatives such as #HaveASafeJourney will open up new avenues to make road safety a people's movement.

I wish all stakeholders success in this noble task. I sincerely hope and pray that the day when no Indian family loses a family member to a road accident will dawn soon.

Nitin Gadkari
Union Minister for Road Transport,
Highways and Shipping
Government of India

A SPECIAL MESSAGE FROM ANAND MAHINDRA

India's record on road safety is shocking by any standards. One person dies every four minutes in road accidents in India. 10 per cent of all road-accident fatalities worldwide, occur in India. More than two lakh people are killed and 12,75,000 people are grievously injured in road accidents in India every year according to the 2015 WHO Global Safety Report. Children are the most vulnerable, with almost sixty children being killed or grievously injured every week. If you add up all the costs of road accidents in India, including loss of life, loss of earnings, medical expenses, property damage and administrative expenses, the monetary loss works out to a stunning one trillion rupees! And that excludes the cost of the loss of love, life and happiness, which is incalculable.

Yes, the statistics are staggering. But their very enormity often renders them meaningless—they just become a number on a page. No statistic can convey the trauma of losing a loved one through an accident. No statistic can communicate the despair of someone whose life has been brought to a standstill due to a road injury. No statistic can console a family that has lost a bread-earner, a parent who has lost a child, a teenager who has lost a beloved sibling or a senior citizen who has lost the support of his old age. To the victims and those who love them, the consequences of a lack of road safety are not just statistics—they are real and wrenching. And, but for the grace of God, the person feeling the impact of those consequences could be you or me.

I am delighted that the Have a Safe Journey initiative drives home this lesson, not through statistics but through stories—stories where the authors put themselves in the shoes of the victims. A recent study concluded that one of the great benefits of reading good literature is that it teaches the reader empathy. The absorbing world of fiction teaches one to understand the emotions and feelings of other people, to see the world through their eyes and feel the world through their hearts. The writers of the stories that you are about to read make you care about people and the human and emotional cost that people pay for ignoring road safety. If these stories strike a chord of empathy in their readers, they will have achieved more than a thousand statistics can.

Because ultimately the responsibility for road safety rests with each one of us. Yes, we need better roads; yes, we need more services; yes, we need better safety standards. But what we need most of all are responsible citizens. Citizens who respect traffic lights, speed limits and the rules of the road. Citizens who uphold the rights of pedestrians. Citizens who adhere to safety regulations, wear helmets, fasten seatbelts, not because there is a cop around the corner but because it can save lives. Citizens who understand that every human life is precious and that they hold the lives of others in their hands.

Fiction often holds up a mirror that shows real life more clearly. I am optimistic that this joint effort by Mahindra Truck and Bus, Natural Habitat Preservation Centre and the Ministry of Road Transport & Highways will do just that, and the result will be a better, safer India.

Anand Mahindra
Executive Chairman
Mahindra Group

PREFACE

Literature, as a form of intellectual culture, has the potential to both entertain and educate. A story can expose readers to different places, time periods, viewpoints and cultures. Through literature, readers can gain experiences they may not otherwise ordinarily have access to.

#HASJ is a project that stems out of our firm belief at NHP Centre that literature can serve as an effective medium to connect and engage with people for promoting awareness, particularly among the youth. Stories can cause deep influence and impressions. There is a pressing need to apply this literary art in promoting awareness about road safety.

Inspiring stories of bravery and humanity often compel people to think more deeply than an advertisement in a newspaper. Similarly, stories of negligence towards road safety norms leading to major upheavals and loss would help people empathies with victims.

This book is a collection of stories selected from the entries of the #HASJ contest. These stories of pain, loss and hope have been edited meticulously and published graciously by Amaryllis, led by the very able Rashmi Menon. This collection will, in all likelihood, be the world's first collection of short stories on road safety issues.

I am grateful to the Ministry of Road Transport and Highways for supporting this initiative. I thank Mahindra Truck and Bus Division for partnering with us in the contest. My thanks also go to members of the jury—Bhupendra Chaubey, Piyush Jha, Rashmi Menon and Brijesh Singh and the pre-jury—Vani Mahesh, Prerana Arora Singh, Soumyadipta Banerjee, Faraaz Kazi and Avijit Ghosal. Richa Thakur and Shruti Bhatt from NHP Centre deserve a pat on their back for implementing #HASJ under the guidance of the #HASJ Steering Committee.

A special thank you to our guest authors, Anand Neelakantan, Ashwin Sanghi, Kiran Manral, Pankaj Dubey, Priyanka Sinha Jha, Shinie Antony and Vikram Kapur, for so kindly agreeing to be a part of this anthology.

Many of these stories have touched me personally and echo in my mind while driving! I hope you too enjoy these stories and these gems stay with you, and every time you are tempted to break a rule, or overlook something important in life and driving, these come back to you with their infectious zeal and will to live and survive.

Happy reading!

Sumant Batra
Founder
Natural Habitat Preservation Centre

A MESSAGE FROM STEERING COMMITTEE MEMBER, TUHIN A. SINHA

Road Safety – It Starts With You!!

Even as I get down to write this piece, comes the sad news of another promising life cut short by a road accident. The victim is India's ace car racer, Ashwin Sunder. Ashwin, while driving his BMW at high speed, along with his wife, hit another car, after which his car crashed into a tree. His car instantly caught fire, charring both Ashwin and his wife. The incident occurred in the wee hours of 18 March 2017 in the heart of Chennai.

When I think of it, a road accident is probably the most unnatural and unpredictable way for a life to end.

The victims of this scourge cut across class, creed and nationality but a majority of them tend to be young. Famous victims include a young cricketing prodigy from India, Dhruv Pandove (died in 1992), a well-known politician, whom many saw as a potential future prime minister, Rajesh Pilot (died in 2000), and Princess Diana (died in 1997). Besides, of course, there are millions of unknown victims whose deaths go unnoticed.

The most tragic thing about road accidents is that it takes only a split second, a moment's lapse of concentration, for it to mark the difference between life and death.

I remember my brush with a road accident nearly twenty-two years ago. It was in 1995. My twelfth standard results had just come out. Buoyed by my good performance, I set out to celebrate with some friends. Driving a Bajaj Super scooter at high speed and with dark glasses on, I wasn't able to spot a speed breaker as it was the same colour as the road. The result was a massive skid: after hitting the speed breaker, the scooter jumped wildly a couple of times and then skidded a good distance away. For a few seconds, I had actually felt I was staring into the face of death and had shut my eyes completely.

I fell off the vehicle and thought I was really badly hurt. But to my pleasant surprise, I only felt a sharp pain from an injury near my elbow. The bruise has left a dark mark till date, even though the wound got healed completely in a few weeks.

When I look back at the accident, I feel certain that it was divine intervention that saved me.

There have been a couple of other occasions where I've had close shaves. For that matter, I am sure most of us who drive regularly have had close shaves or been involved in an accident at some point of time or the other. In fact, every time I read about a ghastly accident, the thought that the next victim could be just about anybody does cross my mind.

If I may make a confession here, in my younger days, I have been guilty of over-speeding. However, over the years, I have sobered down and now make a conscious effort to not exceed prescribed speed limits. In hindsight, the only advice I can give readers is this: Not everybody is lucky to get away with over-speeding, drunken driving or using cell phones while driving. Hence, it helps to be safe than sorry especially since road accidents can involve more than one person, and definitely impact your near and dear ones.

In January 2016, when I was asked by the Honourable Minister, Shri Nitin Gadkari to help his ministry expedite some road-safety initiatives, I knew it was a God-sent opportunity for me to do my bit for a cause I felt strongly about. I will remain grateful to NHP Centre for conceiving the idea of #HaveASafeJourney and to Mahindra Truck and Bus Division for readily sponsoring it. Being a facilitator and a supervisor on this noble project has been an immensely fulfilling experience.

As the Honourable Minister has rightly written in his foreword, literature has a key role to play in making road safety a mass movement.

To be realistic, in a country of the size of India with its high vehicular density, it is virtually impossible to achieve a record of zero accidents or zero fatalities. But the challenge is to see how we can reduce the losses.

As we mull over solutions and work on strategies, I'd like to make some quick observations.

It's a little strange that in our country, the need for kids to wear helmets has been ignored. Parents themselves don't consider it important and somehow believe that by holding their kids tight on a two-wheeler, they can shield them from injury. This is a wrong conception. The Ministry for Road Transport and Highways has made efforts to encourage the use of helmets for kids. Not only must there be a change in the attitude of parents, there is a need for mass manufacture of these helmets. The government is also making efforts to encourage and popularise car seats for kids. A parent should also realise the importance of these safety measures and be absolutely uncompromising on them.

Personally, I have always found technology to be a double-edged sword. While GPS navigation has made travel a lot easier, often I have noticed that on cluttered city roads and especially at intersections, GPS instructions can be confusing, at times resulting in confused movement in the middle of the road. This can result in accidents.

Of course, while we cannot do away with technology, new technology demands new safeguards and at times, increased vigilance.

Finally, I'd like to share a slightly radical idea to invoke road safety consciousness among the masses. I have lately come across online petitions calling for India to have its own National Sex Offenders' Registry. Can we similarly think of a National Traffic Offenders' Registry where anybody who has been booked twice or more for a traffic violation gets listed? In fact, our respective state governments can take the lead here and explore this on an experimental basis. Naming and shaming often works. Besides, irresponsible road behaviour should be a disincentive for job seekers.

If we really want to imbue road safety in our national conscience, we need to link it with the responsibilities of a good citizen. It won't be a bad idea to have dialogues that focus on the importance of road safety in all colleges of the country. Students should be asked to take a road-safety pledge. Ideally, we must raise the pitch of our road-safety campaign to a point where we aggressively promote a road-safety badge, which every vehicle would be expected to sport on the road. The badge would read: I am a responsible Indian. I drive safe.

This kind of personal ownership, even if it is not inherent but created with persuasion, can yield path-breaking results.

As we grapple for innovative and sustainable solutions

in our continued efforts to improve road safety, I feel proud of this little collection of stories on road safety that we've managed to put together. I do hope #HaveASafeJourney will set a new trend of alternative communication solutions to the problem of road accidents in India, where literature plays a pivotal role. Every single life matters and even if this initiative succeeds in saving just one life, the effort would not go in vain.

Tuhin A. Sinha
Author, Content Strategist, Politician

PUBLISHER'S NOTE

For a publisher, it is indeed rare to be able to bring out a book that helps nurture new talent while working for a very important social cause. #HaveASafeJourney (#HASJ) is a project that has given us a chance to do both. Let us tell you a bit about this wonderful initiative. #HASJ is an ambitious road-safety campaign initiated by the Natural Habitat Preservation (NHP) Centre and the Mahindra Truck and Bus Division (MTBD), strongly supported by the Ministry of Road Transport and Highways. As part of this campaign, in mid 2016, the NHP Centre held a contest titled #HASJ, in which participants were asked to send stories on road safety, on themes such as how breaking traffic rules isn't considered heroic, infrastructural failures, futuristic ideas, the role of good Samaritans, etc.

Out of the many entries we received, the very best have been chosen to be a part of this book.

Every story in this book will make you sit up and think. They'll pounce on you every time you even *think* of ignoring the seat belt sign or not putting on your helmet. They'll creep up from behind and put a check on that adrenaline rush you get whenever you exceed speed limits. They'll stare at your face when you're thinking of giving in to your children's demand for a car or a bike before they turn eighteen. They'll ensure you park your vehicle before answering that 'important' call on your cell phone. They will make you respect that traffic policeman standing in the middle of the road, managing rush hour. And all this not through preachy sermons and boring rendering of rules, but through the little gems we call short stories.

For us at Team Amaryllis and Manjul, #HASJ has been a most special project for more reasons than one. Firstly, we are sure that nobody in our team will ever break a traffic rule. And more importantly, it has made us realise how important it is to stand up and take the initiative to change our world. It is easy to sit in the comfort of our homes, read heart-wrenching accounts of accidents, feel bad for the victims for a few minutes and then forget about it. But do we think of what each one of us can do to prevent accidents? Not always.

As the publisher, we feel grateful to have been given the opportunity to join not one but three such teams who are putting their heart and soul into making our roads safer. We would like to thank Shri Nitin Gadkari and the Ministry of Road Transport and Highways for being the wind beneath the wings of this project. Every time we read reports of wonderful initiatives taken by Shri Gadkari's ministry (which is quite often), we feel very proud to be associated with them in a small but significant way. A special thanks to Tuhin A. Sinha, the cog in the wheel of this huge project, for being such a wonderful source of support and practical advice.

A big thank you to Anand Mahindra and the Mahindra Truck and Bus Division for spearheading positive changes to make Indian roads cleaner and safer. It is because of you that this book will perhaps reach places where usual publishing routes cannot even think of venturing. We are extremely grateful for your overwhelming kindness and generosity. Much obliged to the patient and very meticulous Rajeev Malik and Atin Moulik at MTBD for every bit of support and assistance throughout this journey.

We are indebted to our esteemed guest authors Anand Neelakantan, Ashwin Sanghi, Kiran Manral, Pankaj Dubey, Priyanka Sinha Jha, Shinie Antony and Vikram Kapur, for so graciously and readily agreeing to be a part of this project. You participation means a lot to us and your stories have made this book even more special.

And lastly, words are not enough to express our gratitude to the NHP Centre, headed by the multi-faceted Sumant Batra and his wonderful team, Richa Thakur and Shruti Bhatt. Thank you, Sumant, for trusting us with this mammoth project. You and your team have been our rock-solid pillars of strength throughout this journey. A heartfelt thank you for your immense and invaluable contribution towards taking care of every big and small detail pertaining to the project, and for making our part of the journey, as the publisher, so smooth and joyful.

Manjul Publishing House and Amaryllis are proud to be associated with #HASJ. It is an honour to be a part of such a wonderful initiative and get the opportunity to publish stories that will succeed in creating fresh perspectives and more importantly, awareness about road safety.

Stories by Our Guest Authors

HIT AND RUN

Anand Neelakantan

THE WORLD'S FIRST HIT-AND-RUN FOLK TALE IS FROM the *Agnipurana*, but the story is pre-Rig Vedic times.

Long, long ago, before history was born, before even stories were born, there lived an Asura king named Thrasadasyu, on the banks of the Saraswathi river. His kingdom was famed across Jumbudweepa for its spectacular palaces, magical fountains and broad avenues lined with flowering and fruit-bearing trees. King Thrasadasyu ruled his kingdom with an equal mix of kindness and firmness and his people were generally very happy. He had won many wars against the Devas and had expanded his kingdom to the mighty Ganges that flowed in the east and the Narmada in the south.

Thrasadasyu had everything in life except a son. He had consulted astrologers, Brahmins, Maharishis, conducted Yajnas and had even gone on pilgrimages on foot, but he and his three queens were not blessed with a child. His charioteer Wyasan was a wise man who knew the ways of the world. He loved his king and was deeply worried that his master was fretting away. Wyasan suggested that King Thrasadasyu appease Agni, the god of fire.

Thrasadasyu and his wives prayed for 1001 days to Agni, who then blessed them with a son. Agni also gave Thrasadasyu a boon that as long as he remained just and truthful, agni would be present in every hearth of his kingdom. It meant that no one would go hungry. Thrasadasyu was ecstatic. What more could a king wish for! He had been blessed with a son who would be as handsome as Agnideva, and his people would never starve.

In due course, a son as resplendent as the morning sun was born. The entire kingdom rejoiced at the birth of this long-awaited heir to the throne. The prince was named Thrayarun, which meant equal to three morning suns. The king and his wives doted on the child and showered him with all the luxuries in the world. Caravans came from all directions carrying exquisite toys, perfumes, gems, gold, pearls and silk garments for the little prince. Gurus were invited from far and wide to give the boy an education.

With all the pampering, Thrayarun started becoming vain and pompous. He became arrogant because of his skill with weapons, the melody in his songs, the power of his club and the richness of his clothes. People started whispering about the prince in hushed tones and most of the gossip was unfavourable. They respected the king and so no one ever mentioned anything to the indulgent parents.

When the prince turned sixteen, the king presented him with a chariot designed by the great engineer of the Asuras, Mayan himself. The queens presented him with three black horses that were faster than the wind. The prince jumped into the chariot and whipped the horses to a gallop. The queens were delighted to see the prince riding so skilfully on the palace grounds, but as Prince Thrayarun started riding at break-neck speed, they got worried. For the first time, the king also realised that his son was not perfect as he thought, that he had a reckless streak. He consoled himself by thinking and hoping that the boy would become wise when he grew older. But as the prince started performing some jaw-dropping stunts with his chariot, the king started getting worried. He called Wyasan, his charioteer, and instructed him not to allow the prince to ride the chariot and make sure he only sat in the rear seat as a prince ought to do.

Prince Thrayarun was not happy with this injunction, but the king's words were final. Wyasan started ferrying the prince around the city streets. Wyasan was a cautious driver and was concerned about the safety of the prince and the condition of the expensive chariot. His caution while riding the chariot made people refer to it as the tortoise wagon of the prince. The damsels in the city stood in the balconies of their homes and laughed at the slow pace at which the fantastic chariot moved. The prince sat in the passenger seat, fuming and cursing. He started exhorting Wyasan to go faster, but when the old man said he had strict instructions from the king to drive cautiously, the prince would abuse him. Naughty urchins started running alongside the chariot, mimicking its slow gait and bursting into peals of laughter when the prince cursed them.

The prince felt humiliated. He could bear the insult no more. He pushed old Wyasan aside and took the reins into his own hands. He whipped the horses to a blistering pace as the chariot shot forward. Men and women on the street screamed and jumped out of the way, terrified, as the chariot raced through, scattering the crowd. The pretty young women clapped their hands in appreciation and the prince's chest swelled with pride. He acknowledged their applause with a wave of his hand and a nod of his head. He used his whip on any unsuspecting pedestrian who dared to come in his way. Wyasan kept pleading with the reckless prince to slow down but the prince lashed out at the old man too.

To show his skill, the prince tilted the chariot and made it run on its right wheel with the left lifted high in the air. Inspired by him, a few other young men came out with their chariots and soon the busy streets of the capital city turned into a race track. A dozen chariots raced against each other but none could match the speed of the prince's chariot. Old Wyasan cowered in the rear, holding on to the seat for dear life.

The prince had left all other chariots far behind. Exhilarated by his victory, he turned around to mock and abuse his rivals. Poor Wyasan pleaded with him to look where he was going, to concentrate on the road, but the prince ignored him. The chariot had left the road and had climbed on to the pavement, but Thrayarun was busy taunting his rivals. Just then a group of Brahmin boys came out from a gurukula. Wyasan screamed when he saw them, leapt from his seat, knocking Thrayarun from the charioteer's seat on to the road. Wyasan pulled the reins as hard as he could but the chariot was moving at such a speed that it did not stop immediately. The momentum carried it towards the boys who screamed and tried to jump out of its way. Alas, there was a blind boy among them, an eight-year-old, who was crushed under the wheels of the chariot.

A crowd assembled soon and they found a weeping Wyasan on the driver's seat and an unconscious prince on the road. They took the lifeless body of the blind Brahmin boy from under the chariot's wheels. The mob was angry and they started lynching poor Wyasan. Soon, the guards of the king arrived and arrested Wyasan. They took the injured prince to the Raja Vaidya.

The parents of the dead boy approached the king, seeking justice. They wanted the person responsible for the death of their son punished as per the Dharma Shastras of Guru Shukracharya. The king was in a dilemma. His spies had informed him of the real story. He knew his son was responsible. If the matter came to a public trial in his sabha, there would be enough witnesses to say that it was Thrayarun who was responsible for the accident. Which would mean that he would have to put his beloved son in jail. The only way to resolve the problem was to plead with Wyasan to take the blame. After all, it was he who was at the reins when the accident happened. The king offered Wyasan's family great riches and lands if they could persuade Wyasan to admit that he was responsible for the death of the boy. But Wyasan insisted that he would only tell the truth.

When the case came up for trial, Wyasan told the entire story as it had unfolded. The guru of the gurukula also insisted that he had seen the prince riding the chariot in a reckless fashion, and that the old charioteer had, in fact, saved many lives by his timely action. But the pretty young ladies who were cheering the prince from their balconies, the young men who were emulating him and those who sought the king's favours, averred that if the prince, who was such a skilled charioteer, had been in the charioteer's seat, such a mishap would have never happened.

The king pronounced his verdict. Though the prince had ridden fast, it was Wyasan who was responsible for the boy's death and therefore, Wyasan was given life imprisonment.

The king decided to celebrate his son's acquittal by holding a feast that same evening. Invitations were sent to all the important men and women in the capital city. After the music and dance programmes were over, the king invited his guests to the dining room. The first few hours were spent discussing matters of the state, but when the wait for the food dragged on interminably, the Brahmin guests started expressing their displeasure.

A panicking king went to the royal kitchen and found that the vegetables were still raw and the meat was yet to be cooked. The cooks were missing. The king became furious and ordered that the cooks be brought back to their jobs immediately. The guards found them hiding behind the huge utensils and dragged them to the king. The cooks fell at the king's feet and cried. They were not able to light the stoves, they said. A cold fear gripped the king. He directed his guards to check whether the fire had gone out of every hearth in the city. The guards returned with the news that the king's fears had indeed come true.

Agni had gone out of the kingdom for Thrasadasyu had punished an innocent man. The king went down on his knees and pleaded for mercy. He ordered Wyasan to be released and Thrayarun to be imprisoned. The soldiers dragged a screaming, howling, cursing and kicking prince away and set Wyasan free. The hearth in the royal kitchen started smoking again and with a flourish the fire started to burn, filling the kingdom with the rich aroma of justice.

Thus, says the *Agni Purana*, the country that denies justice to the poor and favours the rich and powerful, will remain poor.

SOMETHING ABOUT MARY

Ashwin Sanghi

It was a pleasant summer day. August was one of the better months of the year with the usual freezing temperatures giving way to warmer comfort and sunshine. But open cars always required that little extra layer of insulation, given the unpredictability of Irish weather, so Mary had placed a blanket on her lap, just in case.

Mary settled into her seat, allowing her mind to wander. The forty-two-year-old had enough to think about. Her privileged upbringing hadn't been easy. That sounded strange but was absolutely true. While she and her sisters had enjoyed every possible comfort at the stately mansion surrounded by manicured lawns and abundant trees, the challenges of breaking into men's bastions as a woman had haunted her for most of her life.

Mary had coped, relying on her innate brilliance. Her naturally scientific mind had pushed her into becoming an avid astronomer. Her cousin, William, had built the world's largest reflecting telescope and Mary had sketched each stage of the process in remarkable detail. She was also interested in entomology, using the microscope that her father had presented her with to catalogue hundreds of insect specimens with exquisitely detailed drawings. She was an exceptionally talented artist and painter, eventually illustrating several books and papers for other writers. Both the microscope and the telescope permitted her to lose herself in a world beyond man-made boundaries.

Mary and her husband, Henry, were staying for a week at William's house in County Offaly in the Midlands of Ireland. The place was huge, castle-like and surrounded by what were considered the tallest hedges in the world. The grounds also sported the world's oldest wrought-iron bridge. Mary loved wandering the grounds along with her children and soaking in the beauty of the surroundings. Each visit was an enjoyable experience, not least because of the fact that her cousin had a scientific temperament just like hers.

Mary didn't quite know at that time that she would be far more famous than any of her cousins. More famous than she could ever imagine.

She was one among a total of three women who were on the mailing list of the Royal Astronomical Society. The other two ladies included the queen. But that would not be the reason for Mary's glory. Nor would her fame emerge from the fact that she had succeeded in self-publishing a book which had proceeded to go into eight reprints—not bad for a girl with no university education.

Neither astronomy nor entomology, publishing success nor artistic talent, would drive her renown.

She sighed as she waited for Henry and the boys to get going. It was almost half past three that Tuesday afternoon and she was getting impatient, fiddling with the blanket on her lap. Eventually they set off with Mary seated in the front seat next to Henry in the shiny red vehicle. Her nephews, Richard and Charles, occupied the rear seats.

Henry was a cautious driver. They made steady progress at an easy pace along the road as they neared the bend by the church. They had covered the route many times and every twist, turn, incline and fork was predictable. What could not have been predicted was a sudden jolt—an unexplainable jerk that made the vehicle shudder. Henry turned leftwards to check if his wife was fine. But she had disappeared. Poof! Gone in the blink of an eyelid.

The next few seconds were a blur. Henry would probably replay every frame of that incident in an infinite loop within his mind for the rest of his life, but it was of no use. Mary was gone and she had become famous in the process—for the wrong reason. Her name would be recorded in history books as the first person who lost her life in a car accident. The day was Tuesday, 31 August 1869.

Mary Ward had been seated in a steam-powered car built by her cousin, William Parsons. Her nephews, Richard and Charles Parsons, had been seated in the back seat. The car had gathered steam and was travelling at moderate speed when it neared the church in Parsonstown. While manoeuvring a sharp bend leading from the Mall into Cumberland Street, the engine had shuddered violently, making Mary lose her balance. She had fallen from the bench seat to the ground. One of the heavy wheels of the vehicle—almost roadroller-like—had passed over her head, dislocating her neck and crushing the bones of her face. She had died almost instantly. She had been carried to the house of Dr Woods whose home was opposite the scene of the accident but it was too late. She was dead on arrival.

Ironically, four years previously the Red Flag Act of 1865 had prescribed a maximum speed limit of four miles per hour for motorcars. This had almost entirely killed the demand for such vehicles but some enthusiasts continued to maintain homemade motorcars like the one William Parsons had assembled. It would be another ten years before Karl Benz was granted a patent for his motorcar powered by an internal combustion engine, and an even longer ninety years before the Ford Motor Company began offering safety seat belts as optional extras.

But before any of that could happen, Mary Ward would enter the annals of history as the unfortunate victim of the first car accident, a distinction that she would have preferred not to have.

SUDDEN BREAK

Kiran Manral

DEBU NATH CRINGED WHEN HE SAW HIS FATHER waiting patiently beside his trusty old Bajaj scooter a little distance from the school gate. He stood at the same spot every day, come rain or shine, one helmet on his head and one dangling from the handlebar of the scooter, for Debu. Debu had tried long and hard to convince his father that he would come home on his own. After all, home was just a short auto ride away from school. Debu's mother was not in favour of Debu taking the school van or the school bus after he'd been bullied mercilessly by a group of seniors in his first week on the bus a couple of years ago. Besides, the school bus took at least forty-five minutes to cover a distance that barely required fifteen minutes. Mrs Nath believed that the time could be spent productively, either eating lunch or completing homework. So Mr Nath, whose bank was fortunately located close to the school, would pick Debu up, take him home, have a piping hot meal himself and then return to office.

Debu's father was a bit of an embarrassment for the boy. He wore his pants hitched high and his shirt buttoned to the collar. Of course his clothes were impeccably ironed, thanks to Mrs Nath's prodigious housekeeping skills, and his hair plastered down with Navratna oil. 'Oil keeps the head cool,' he would tell Debu whenever Debu tried to talk him out of the practice. Perhaps there was some merit in what he said, but the perfume of the preferred oil overpowered the generous sprayings of the strongly fragrant deodorant his father liked to use. Debu's father was always cool. Not Xavier D'Costa's father's kind of cool. He was a Bollywood choreographer of no mean repute and sported a hip-hop style and street cred. And yet, Debu was grateful for his father's unflappable cool, especially during report card time.

Debu waited until all his friends had dispersed, then walked up to where Baba stood, a calm Buddha-like smile playing on his face. He had never seen his father lose his temper ever, except perhaps on the rare occasion, but his mother more than made up for it. Even when his mother was in full spate, and neighbours peered in from their adjoining balconies to check if there was murder and mayhem in the offing, his father would remain calm, smiling through it all. Sometimes Debu thought his father smiled solely to get a rise out of his mother who was endemically short-tempered and had an average of one blowout per week, which had the ceiling fans shake when she was in full airing of her larynx and the plaster rain down from the ceiling. It was a miracle he and Baba hadn't suffered permanent hearing loss yet.

Debu put on the helmet his father handed to him, and was about to climb onto the scooter when a car passed them by, the music blaring loud enough to put the beat back into a corpse's heart. He turned around and saw Aman Shroff, a grade nine student and a year senior to Debu. He was the designated Richie Rich of the school and the sigh of every girl's heart in Debu's class.

Everyone in school knew Aman. Aman was dropped and picked up every single day in a fancy chauffeur-driven car. He was so good looking that he had already decided his calling to be a hero in Bollywood. He attended school half-heartedly, studying just enough to keep his father off his back. He was a happy-go-lucky soul, with none of the airs that generally afflicted kids who came from exceedingly rich families. As his car drove past Debu, Aman waved out to him from the sunroof where he usually stood. He envied Debu's ability to be at the top of the class every term without being a bookworm just as Debu looked enviously at Aman's liveried chauffeur and fancy car. He wished he had the swag that came from confidence as Aman had, knowing he would be taken care of, no matter what he did.

'Baba,' Debu said loudly, in order to be heard over the traffic and the helmet. 'Why don't you buy a car? A small one? Everyone in my class has a car.' His father was silent. Debu continued in a rush. 'And it will be good during the monsoon, I won't get wet, and you won't either. It's so hot nowadays, I feel like taking off this helmet and throwing it away.'

His father slowed down, turned on the indicator, went on to give a hand signal to the vehicles behind him, to further confirm that he was indeed moving to the left, and stopped near the pavement. He got off, propped the scooter up on its stand, removed his helmet and stared at Debu. His eyes were blazing. Debu had rarely seen his father angry before.

'Are you ashamed of travelling on a scooter, Debu?' his father asked, his voice soft, very soft. Debu knew that when his father's voice went very soft he was angry.

'No, Baba,' Debu was slightly abashed at his own selfishness. After all, Baba didn't even buy himself a new pair of shoes until the pair he was using hadn't completely fallen apart, beyond the emergency resuscitation capabilities of the cobbler at the end of their lane. 'It was just a thought.'

'I will buy a car, Debu,' Baba said, looking into his eyes. 'But not now. I am saving for your education. First, I must be sure that I will be able to pay for whatever stream of education you choose. Only then will I buy a car. Do you know how much one needs to pay just to get admission into engineering or medical?'

Debu nodded. 'Until then, I am sorry, you must come with me on the scooter. When you grow up and become an engineer, you buy me a car and drive me around.' Baba laughed, his easy booming laugh. The moment of anger was over. Debu's cool unflappable Baba was back. 'And put that helmet back on, Debu,' he said. 'I will not have you on the scooter without the helmet.'

Debu grumbled about the heat and the rash beginning around his neck but put the helmet on without further ado. As he clambered back on, he noticed that a small patch at the back of the scooter had begun rusting.

As they approached the major intersection through much traffic before turning towards the lane that led to their home, the road cleared up for a bit. A car overtook them on the right. It was Aman Shroff standing out through the sunroof, arms outstretched, looking pretty much like Leonardo Di Caprio in *Titanic*. They must have got held up in the traffic behind, traffic that the humble scooter had cut through.

If only they had a car, Debu thought, even one without a sunroof or a liveried chauffeur! But his father was prosaic and practical, and he would probably have to wait until he earned his own money to buy one himself.

Then it happened. A small boy darted across the open road. Baba swerved precariously although the boy was quite a distance away. There was the sickening screech of brakes being slammed from a little ahead to their right, a dull thud and a split second later, a scream that pierced Debu's heart. The traffic came to a halt, people rushed to the spot. Everything was a blur to Debu. He felt things were happening around him in slow motion.

Baba took the scooter to the side of the road and parked it carefully. Debu took off his helmet, trying to see what had happened through the throng assembled. Aman Shroff's car had crashed into the divider and spun around. The front of the car was crumpled, and smoke rose from the bonnet. The driver had had a miraculous escape and was out in the thick of the crowd, trying to fight his way through to whatever lay there. Aman was nowhere to be seen. Debu's heart began to pound in his chest. A sudden queasiness welled up in his throat. 'Baba,' he pulled his father's sleeve in panic, 'has anyone died?'

Baba, calm and measured as always, said, 'I don't think so, but why don't you wait right here, and I'll go and check. Don't move from here, okay.' There was little likelihood of that. Wild horses couldn't drag him away, he was fascinated and terrified of what he might see.

'Yes, Baba,' Debu replied obediently, although half of him was itching to tear across the road ignoring the cacophony of horns and voices demanding that a passage be cleared to allow others to pass through, never mind that an accident had just happened; the other half told him he was best standing at the side, rather than poking his nose into the crowd and seeing things that could be the stuff of bad dreams for months to come.

'Damn sad, yaar,' said a voice from behind him. Debu didn't turn around immediately though the voice seemed familiar and yet unfamiliar. He was still trying to look through the throng of people to figure out what had happened. If it was anything gruesome, he could recount it at length in school the next day.

'Good thing your dad drives so carefully, and you had your helmet on. I wish I'd listened to my mum and stayed inside the car instead of standing halfway out like that and insisting Gopal chacha drive fast.'

Debu started and turned back to see who was speaking to him. There was no one there, just a faint flickering that could well have been waves of heat rising from the asphalted road.

CAR POOL

Pankaj Dubey

THE RUCKSACK HANGING ON HER BACK WAS HALF-mouth-open. Her white-sleeved shirt hung from the bag like a kite's tail. She was running away from Mumbai... again! Just as she had done three months ago. In the same pajamas and kaftan. Restlessly she waited for her train at the ugly Kurla station. She wanted to forget everything—Mumbai, the Goa Highway... everything! And yes, the car pool!

Three months ago, when the nip in the air was flirtatious enough and Mumbai's landscape was welcoming the oncoming winter, Avni had decided to go to Goa for the Hippie Music Festival. It was the 'broke week' of the month, but the fact that she had only about ₹5400 in her savings account did not deter her from planning her trip.

'Anjuna's night market. You have seen, na? My friend's bungalow is there... I have asked her. You can share a room with her servant, for free,' teased Avni's friend Natasha on Snapchat.

'Nuts, is this your way of helping me or are you mocking my impoverished state or showing your insensitivity towards the poor servant or being sarcastic at my impromptu plan?' retorted Avni.

'Twenty per cent of each of the listed categories,' laughed Natasha while simultaneously beating the instant coffee and sugar mix in a cup.

'Mom has sent an NRI mumma's boy. He is coming with his mother to see me tomorrow afternoon. Before they arrive, I have to escape!' Avni had almost packed her bag.

'Means you are disobeying your mom?'

'Not disobeying her. Obeying my heart,' smiled Avni as she zipped the rucksack.

'How will you go? Bus?' asked Natasha while removing her contact lenses.

'*Tripping Together*, a car pool app.' Avni looked all sorted.

'Be careful, woman! Don't do these stupid things,' Natasha warned.

'You silly girl, apply for the post of a warden... You should not be a designer,' Avni waggled her tongue. 'Now bye, coochie poo!'

It was 10 p.m. Avni made a salami sandwich for herself and sat in her balcony which overlooked the sea. She fiddled with the Tripping Together app, and surfed for people offering rides to Goa. She was looking for a guy without a moustache and price capped for not more than ₹500.

She managed to find a car ride offer from an Andheri guy, Suyash Ray. Both the car and the owner looked great. Tall, sturdy and good-looking. She immediately sent a request and in a matter of seconds, got a confirmation from Suyash. The pick-up point was Juhu Circle at 7 a.m.

Avni had to wait for a good twenty-five minutes for Suyash to arrive. He was chivalrous enough to open the car door but Avni did not like such treatment.

'You look better than your DP… take it as a compliment,' joked Avni as she settled down in the front seat.

'Seatbelt,' said Suyash in a matter-of-fact tone. 'It is your security guard, remember?' he added after a minute, noticing her casual attitude towards the warning.

'You are like a "Hero ka baap"… the very strict type,' Avni tried to lighten the mood.

'Can you please strap on the seat belt? It's very distracting,' said Suyash in a stern voice.

'I will behave,' smiled Avni as she obeyed.

The drive had begun. They kept switching radio stations till they could negotiate a common taste in music. Both loved Rahman. Afterwards, for quite some time, Avni's phone kept ringing.

'Why aren't you answering that call?' asked Suyash.

'Want to stay away from marriage. Mom has arranged for an NRI guy to come and meet me tomorrow. I plan to run away before the boy and his family reach Mumbai.'

'How mean of you to do this to your mother!'

'I mean no harm to anybody but I am in no mind

space to get married. I thought I will go to Goa for a week to attend the Hippie Music Festival.'

'Where do you work?' asked Suyash after a brief spell of silence.

'I am a wedding photographer.'

'God, I never thought I will ferry a crazy stupid girl,' Suyash said half seriously.

'Hey, I am paying you for this,' reminded Avni. 'So now you tell me. What do you do?'

'I look after my dad's business—export of exotic spices. I source some from Goa,' Suyash smiled.

'Ohho, the spice connoisseur! I am really bad at identifying two things, masala and guys, both!' giggled Avni, gathering her hair into a loose bun. Suyash laughed too and thus followed an easy conversation about everything under the sun.

The two strangers opened up to each other and talked about their lives and funny incidents from the past. The frequent chai and loo breaks made them bond like old friends.

Goa was about 120 kilometres away. They stopped near a river to see the sunset. It looked like a painting. The sun seemed half-dipped in the sea.

'Let's kiss the sun,' suggested Avni.

'You are crazy!' Suyash looked positively embarrassed.

'No, actually, it's fun. Come na,' she pulled him to the riverbank. Suyash felt his skin tingle at her touch.

The rays of the sun danced on the calm surface of the water. Avni bent down to kiss the river and the ripples caressed her lips.

She gestured to Suyash to imitate her. Though he found it funny, he did follow her.

'You are not a good kisser,' Avni laughed.

Suyash moved closer to her.

'Aren't you too judgemental?' he asked, looking into her eyes.

Their eyes did not flutter even for a second. They looked deep into each other's eyes. Suyash was as calm as the river. His arms circled her, gathering her against him in a warm embrace. They kissed each other with sun-kissed lips.

The journey bridged sunrise and sunset. The twelve hours together felt magical.

Goa was now just forty-five kilometres away. The car pool ride would soon come to an end. They would go in their separate directions.

The drive had been long and both were feeling drowsy by now.

Suyash opened his car's boot. He had a bottle of wine tucked snugly in his bag.

'To our one-car stand!' Suyash laughed as he held the bottle high in the air.

They both guzzled from the bottle.

'Can I drive?' asked Avni.

'Do you?' Suyash was possessive about his car.

'Trust this stranger.' Avni took the keys and hopped into the driver's seat. Suyash sat beside her.

'Seatbelt,' he reminded her again.

'No school-teacher mode, please! We are free birds,' she said firmly and rolled down the window.

'You are disobeying the rules,' cautioned Suyash.

'I am obeying my heart.' Avni revved up the car's engine.

'Keep to the speed limit,' Suyash looked scared.

'The sky should be our limit!' Avni stepped on the accelerator and started speeding.

The adrenaline rush gave her a high. Her hair flew wildly around her face. Suyash tucked whatever he could gather of her hair behind her ears.

Both were in the throes of new-found love.

'Are you commitment phobic?' Suyash asked suddenly.

'Are you checking if I am marriage material? Don't do that. I am running away to avoid getting married,' Avni warned.

'Poor guy, he is coming to see you tomorrow and you are running to some Goa hippie festival.' Suyash took off his sunglasses. It had become a little dark.

Avni was still on her ecstasy ride, playing with the accelerator.

The car was speeding at 150 kilometres per hour when out of nowhere a white SUV came from the opposite direction. Within a fraction of a second, the two cars crashed into each other. Avni and Suyash lost consciousness.

Black. Grey. Red. The two unconscious bodies lay covered in the colours of a highway mishap.

Miraculously, the guy driving the SUV had escaped with minor scratches. He took both Avni and Suyash to the hospital.

By the time they reached the hospital, Suyash had regained his consciousness. He had multiple injuries on his body. But just because he had had his seatbelt on, his state wasn't as bad as Avni's. Avni was in a coma. She had suffered a major concussion.

Suyash was in tears. He thanked the guy who got them there.

'I am Vishal, we are from Texas. My mom, my sister and I were on a holiday in Goa. We were on our way to meet someone in Mumbai. And this happened. What's the name of the lady with you?' asked Vishal in his Americanised accent.

'Avni,' replied Suyash.

'Oh, even the name of the girl I am going to meet is Avni! She is a wedding photographer.'

Suyash stopped breathing for a moment.

'Hope she gets well soon... is she your wife?' asked Vishal, matter-of-factly.

Suyash was still in a daze. He could not process what he had just heard. Vishal's words went into a hollow well inside him. He felt his head spin, as though a whirlpool had suddenly inhabited it.

Was it the morphine, the sedatives or the cruel

coincidence? Avni and Suyash's lives had crossed the speed limit and lost grip. The momentary joy had got busted and scattered two lives.

A car pool had changed their lives. The romance could have bloomed, the inner conflicts could have dissolved, the journey could have been completed! Sadly, the steering of life had lost its direction.

RUSH HOUR

Priyanka Sinha Jha

DAMN! THE DOORBELL RANG FOR THE NTH TIME that morning. First it was the maid, then the bhajiwala, the dhobi and now the landlord along with the building contractor, had just announced himself at the door.

'I waited all of yesterday, but he *had* to come right now!' she fumed inside her head. Standing in her pajamas, she mustered a fake smile as the garrulous old landlord and the contractor tramped around looking for damp patches in every nook and cranny of the small one-bedroom apartment.

The hands of the clock were pointing to half past nine, which meant that she had exactly thirty minutes to wash her hair, iron out the creases in her outfit, get the maid out and leave. She had an important presentation at eleven o'clock in office and couldn't afford to be late. No time to spare for niceties.

Finally, when the duo walked towards the door, she sighed audibly, rudely slamming the door on them.

Hurriedly ticking off the items on her to-do list, Shweta was ready within the scheduled half hour. And then she remembered that the driver had called in sick. Was it a sign or a portent that her presentation would be a disaster?

Muttering under her breath, she booked herself a cab, which promised to arrive within five minutes. She requested the cab driver to pick her up from the coffee shop across the road so that the long U-turn to the main road from her apartment block could be avoided. 'A couple of minutes saved will go a long way,' she thought.

◆

That was the thought to which Shweta opened her eyes. There was an agonising pain on the left side of her head, her mouth was dry, and even in her barely conscious haze, she could feel her thumb throb.

'How do you feel?' someone asked.

Shweta tried to bring her mind to focus and answer. Some sort of a guttural, garbled sound escaped her lips. She wanted to tell the voice that she had a presentation to make. But darkness engulfed her.

Thoughts ebbed and flowed dreamlike in her head. She felt as though her body was floating, weightlessly. But the pain stayed, constant and continuous. The next few days remained the same and it was almost a fortnight before two of the voices around her became recognisable. Papa's and Mamma's.

What were they doing here? What had happened to her presentation?

In days that followed, Shweta drifted in and out of her comatose state before recovering consciousness. Doctor Madaan, the neurologist at the hospital, declared her out of danger but said that recovery was a long way off. Shweta stole a glimpse in the mirror while Mamma was brushing her unruly hair one morning. Her jaw dropped in horror. Her normally cherubic face looked hideous. Her mouth was pulled to one side, one of her eyes would not shut and had to be taped down to prevent it from getting an infection. That concussion on her head had been nasty; the blood clot in her brain had paralysed half her face. There was partial memory loss too. Alternating between pain and perplexity, Shweta wanted to scream.

Nothing seemed to make sense, till one day, two policemen dropped in for a visit.

'Madam, what happened?' asked the senior of the two.

Shweta shrugged in reply.

'Witnesses ke hisab se, aap road cross kar rahi thi. Udhar se gaadi ne thok diya. Par gaadi wala mila nahin. (According to witnesses, you were hit by a car while crossing the road. We haven't found the driver yet),' the havaldar volunteered.

Shweta stared at him disbelievingly.

The havaldar, Mr Kamble, coughed self-consciously, and spoke again. 'Madam, aage se khali phukat ghai-ghai nahi karne ka (next time don't rush about unnecessarily).'

Anger suddenly raged within her at this patronising advice. 'Main kaam ke liye jaldi mein thi par tumko nahin samajh ayega (I was hurrying to work but you won't understand),' Shweta slurred back her first words as saliva dripped from her drooping mouth. The policemen nodded sympathetically and left.

For the next few days, all Shweta could think about was the callous bastard who had done this to her. Who could he be? She kept trying to put together pieces of the puzzle till her head hurt, but no answers were forthcoming.

'There is no need to panic,' Dr Madaan, sensing Shweta's frustration, reassured her. 'Such symptoms are common among accident-trauma victims.'

Shweta heard out the neurologist with characteristic impatience before collapsing onto the hospital bed that she was growing so weary of. He obviously did not understand Shweta's misery. With no recall of the incident, how would she bring the culprit to book?

Tears squeezed out through the taped-down eye. Shweta had missed the big presentation and yes, someone else had filled in for her. It would be some time before she could put together the pieces of her life while the rogue driver roamed guilt-free. Life was certainly not fair.

A few silent minutes later, her mother said, 'Look at the bright side. You are alive.' Then with a smile, she added, 'Besides, you must admit, the one-eyed pirate look kind of suits your grumpy mood.'

She looked at her mother and forced a feeble smile. Mamma's words gave her a little hope. She needed that. Once again she signalled that she wanted to go to the bathroom. Using a bedpan was an easier option but she preferred to drag herself to the loo with Mamma's support and the nurse holding up the drip bottle.

While returning from the loo expedition, she noticed a man talking to Papa in the corridor outside her room. He looked familiar. She had seen him around in the hospital.

As if on cue, Dr Madaan came into the room, smiling cheerfully. 'I think there is some good news in store,' he announced triumphantly after a quick examination of her eyes and a glance through the reports. 'You can expect to be discharged tomorrow.'

This was good news indeed. Shweta was about to sit up but he motioned for her to lie still.

'There is someone you should meet.' He asked the nurse to call in Shweta's father and the man along with him.

'Beta, this is Mr Gaurav Tejani who brought you to the hospital,' Papa explained.

Overcome with emotion, Shweta felt tears trickling down her cheeks.

'Mr Tejani, I am not smiling because it might scare you but thanks for saving my life,' she said, making light of her situation.

Mr Tejani flashed an apologetic smile. Papa hurriedly launched into an account of how Mr Tejani had brought her in and had refused to leave till they were safely by her side.

'If not for him, you would have died or lapsed into a coma,' Papa informed her yet again to emphasise the point.

'Mr Tejani, could you please tell me what exactly happened? The cops have no clue,' Shweta pleaded, her voice trembling with anticipation.

'Shweta ji,' he said with an air of formality as though addressing a VIP, 'It was my car that hit you.'

Shweta was stunned into silence.

As though divining her thoughts, Tejani started speaking again. 'But before you jump to any conclusions, let me give you the complete picture. I had an urgent meeting with an investor from Hong Kong. He had to rush to the airport and I was running late. The road to the hotel was jammed so I jumped the traffic signal and before I knew it, my car had hit you!'

His words left Shweta speechless. The missing pieces from her memory began to fall in place. She had stepped on the road outside her building gate and was checking the text message from the cab service while crossing the road.

Shweta was too exhausted to scream a few expletives at him so she just sank back into the hospital bed.

Tejani squeezed in a last few words, 'Please understand that it really was a very unfortunate accident. In order to make amends I chose to try and save you instead of bribing my way out of this. Now, I leave it to you. If you would like me to go and surrender myself to the police I will do so.'

'What audacity,' she thought to herself as she processed Tejani's startling revelation. He was obviously trying to buy her support.

There was an awkward silence.

Papa's voice broke through, 'What's important is that Shweta is fine.'

Watching Shweta's face go ashen at Papa's statement, Dr Madaan chimed in, 'I think we have had enough disclosure for today. Please come back tomorrow, Mr Tejani.'

Once her shock had subsided, she went over Tejani's words again and again. 'How could Tejani think I would spare him?'

Shweta had a sleepless night, mulling over every possible scenario—from sending Tejani to jail or slapping him hard till his face was paralysed. Somewhere, in the wee hours of the morning she came to a decision.

A while later, Shweta woke up to a flurry of activity around her. Mamma was packing her things into bags and Papa was signing forms. True to his promise, Dr Madaan had discharged her. Her spirits lifted immediately. On their way out, Shweta bid a fond farewell to the doctor who had kept up her morale through the ordeal.

Once they were all seated comfortably in the car, Papa revved the engine. The car was about to start moving when Tejani suddenly appeared by the side of her window. Without as much as a greeting, he anxiously asked, 'What have you decided, Shweta ji? Are you going to make a police case?'

Shweta gave him a long look. Unshaven and dishevelled, he, too, had obviously not slept well. She fished out what looked like a prescription from her handbag, thrust the paper in Tejani's hand, and signalled Papa to drive away.

Tejani opened the paper in his hand with trembling fingers. There was just one line scrawled across the page, 'Aage se khaali phukat ghai-ghai nahin karne ka!'

As the car drove away, Shweta chuckled to herself imagining the expression on Tejani's face.

WHY WE DON'T TALK

Shinie Antony

Are we what they call the hi-bye types? Because this is it, I guess. Can't believe you are no one I used to know and doesn't look like we'll bump into each other again. This pebble in my hand... wish I could send it skimming over the pond near your childhood home. Where you played all by yourself because your mother died when you were two and your grandmother was busy in the kitchen.

You spoke to imaginary friends—perhaps you sensed me even then, though I was born ten years after you—and were excited by most things they said in return. You shared your secrets with the pillow, into which you sobbed when your father did not come to school the day you won a prize for topping your class. You soon lost interest in academics but achieved success in what was just a hobby—keeping fit. Your fear of death was there from the beginning and, like most people, you knew you'd die someday. So you ran marathons and swam and joined karate classes and opened a gym of your own. You are thin, yes, but jam-packed with muscles. A wiry body and a ready laugh. Of course, girls flock to your gym and want to meet you outside it. They call you handsome and though you shrug in a cool way, you want to elope with each one of them.

Everything about you became tight-fitting—jeans, wallet, days, nights, your whole solar system. You worked, you played, backpacked through Leh, picked up a guitar and followed G minor.

I was born by then, and living a doll's life. My parents had tried to conceive for years and got me on their third IVF, which mutilated my dad's bank balance and my mother's sense of humour. They overreacted to me from the moment I was made.

I never wore a frock twice. Feeding me and entertaining me was all my mother ever wanted to do. I was watched keenly for any talent, and every picture I sketched and clay monstrosity I sculpted will live on in my mother's showcase forever. That is how she will grow old—before she forgets her bearings and existence, before dementia takes its toll and turns her memories into papier-mâché—staring unblinkingly at all my early arts and crafts.

The first milk tooth I lost is set amidst diamonds in my father's ring, shifted from finger to finger as he swelled over the years. He says the happiness of having me has given him a potbelly all over. Rubies cup my milk teeth in marmalade chandeliers Mother wears in her ears only on grand occasions.

Remember when you, with a heart beating fast, agreed to meet Sharu's mom alone? That was the first time you touched a woman and you wanted to lick her all over, puppy-like, although you couldn't stop calling her Aunty. She was, after all, Sharada's mom, and when you visited her home, Aunty made tea for you until the day she rested, deliberately, her foot on yours, and you met her eye in a new way.

You were useless in the back of her SUV, though your body—the body you believe in so implicitly to obey commands and do what you want it to do and be what you want it to be—went away all on its own, surprising you with its mind, will and total lack of morals. It will take you a while to go back to that excitement, after me I mean, but life's little madnesses will get you again...

Verse will approach at night
Urgent, in a mood to fight
You must pretend to give in
To paranormal bits of djinn

How proud you were when you bought your first car, this after having fought so hard with your dad for the scooter he gave you when you grumbled about bus rides being tedious.

'Buy it with your own money,' he had snapped, and fury frizzed your hair.

You got this second-hand Santro two weeks ago. You lived in it, dreamt of it at night and baby-talked to it.

When you met me that first time we did not look at each other. We are a circumspect two, cosy in our own orbits, and perhaps schoolgirls are not eye-catching enough for you. But the second time, our eyes did meet. You screeched your car to a halt and glared at me.

I had glared right back, as daddy calls me Shehzadi and I can do no wrong.

Then you made a sound, a disgusted sound, which rarely (rarely!) comes my way, and reversed and drove away. I stared at the back of your car, happy with its dent and dust. You didn't deserve any better, I thought smugly and went my way, never to think of you again until now. Until this minute.

I had finished talking to a friend, come to the road and then charged into the bus stop again to tell her something I'd just remembered. My feet slowly backed into the road and, because my eyes were still on her, I saw my friend's face change from sweetness to slow and sticky panic. It filled her face to the full, this panic, but before the meaning of such dread could communicate itself to me, I began to arc.

I saw my shoes walk the sky. Something warm splashed on my face and turned cold in an instant. A question fluted within, vanished. My fingers were the last thing I felt; they crawled out like flies from under me and clawed at mud. One hand clenched this pebble while the other fluttered once, twice, and then lay down quietly.

Now our hands are touching for the first time. Your hand is red with my blood. A flat and opaque blood, still clumsy from travelling my veins, too surprised to clot. You know, even as you scream, that I am no more, that my breath, my being, my life and laugh are all things of the past. You remember yesterday. You remember making that disgusted face and feel more ashamed of that than this. For this is senseless and will not make sense to you or anybody else for a long while.

My parents will arrive before the police or medical personnel as they live within walking distance. Before that my friend will reach home shaking, and ring my doorbell with all the suppressed fear I saw on her face, and finish none of her sentences. She will need sleeping pills well into adulthood. But she will also seduce many men with her post-me vulnerability. I am the anecdote of her lifetime, what blows up her eyes, hares off her heartbeat and trembles her alphabets. Two marriages later, she will forget me somewhat.

My parents, waiting to have lunch with me, will leave the TV on to come here, dishevelled and disbelieving, almost amused in their utter contempt of such a happening and a hundred per cent confident of my immortality, and sit to my left and right and interfere with anybody who wants to move my body. Love will make such a nuisance of them. People who make you suffer from a unique arrogance; they presume they will go before you.

And they will ask me over and over again, 'Why are you lying here on the road, beta?'

My bed at home has roseate ruffles and a Barbie theme my mother saw in a foreign magazine. When the stretcher shifts me, they will demand small heart-shaped cushions for my head and ankles. They will say loudly that that is how I sleep, *always*. My mother will ask Dad to run home and get the cushions, but he won't be able to take his eyes off my face and from then on, quite simply, their moments of fact and fiction will never coincide. Barred entry into the ambulance along with me, they will shove violently at those around and finally be sedated.

Surrounded by policemen and the family-friend lawyer your father has rushed to the spot, you stand at a distance, still unspeaking, still not guilty, still dazed about the why and where and who of me.

(This story first appeared in the book *Why We Don't Talk*, an anthology of short stories edited by Shinie Antony, and published by Rupa.)

THE LEVEL CROSSING

Vikram Kapur

If you dubbed the white Xylo cab and its driver Satish a pair of vagabonds who hadn't washed in days, you wouldn't be that far from the truth. For three days and three nights, the Xylo and its driver had been on the move. They had spent the days ferrying staff and executives from businesses in Noida and Greater Noida to meetings in Delhi and back. At night, they had worked at the call centres in Gurgaon, transporting employees from their homes all over the National Capital Region to their workstations, and, soon after dawn, taken the same employees, who were now exhausted after a night of affecting American accents in order to speak to strangers on the other side of the globe, home to their beds.

In the past, Satish would park his cab outside a call centre and sprawl on one of the seats to catch up on sleep while his passengers pretended to be George, John or Annie on a telephone line. For the last three nights, that had not been possible. No sooner had he dropped off the call centre employees than he was rushing to pick up clients looking to catch flights from the Indira Gandhi International Airport. Normally, he would have heeded his protesting limbs and turned at least some of them down in favour of sleep. But these days he had to take on all the work he could get. His sister's marriage had just been finalised, and he and his father, a farmer in western UP, were scrambling to cobble together the money required to stage the wedding and pay the dowry. The wedding was a mere four weeks away, hence the need to keep going without pause. He had been reduced to catnapping, smoking beedis, chewing on paan, and downing bottles of water in a bid to stay awake. Even if he'd had the time to wash the Xylo, his spent body wouldn't have let him. By the third day, he couldn't even spare the energy to wipe it down. The closest he himself had come to a bath in all that time was dousing his face with water in a bid to prevent his eyes from closing. By the third day, he could have passed for a vagabond with his scraggly face, his lank hair, and his damp clothes reeking of sweat. The Xylo looked a little better, with dust and grime staining its exterior and mud streaking its tyres.

That afternoon, Satish and his cab were taking a group of professors to their homes in south Delhi from a new university that had opened outside Greater Noida. Their regular driver, who was ill, had asked Satish to fill in for him. None of the professors appeared pleased with the arrangement. The English professor, who normally sat in front with the driver, took one look at Satish and wrinkled his nose, before retreating to the back of the cab. The Sociology professor commented on the empty plastic bottles strewn all over the cab and refused to get in until Satish got rid of them. The Biology professor walked round the cab, inspecting it as if it were a specimen under her microscope, before climbing in reluctantly. The Political Science professor wondered aloud as to whether the regular driver was really ill or was using illness as an excuse not to come to work, like so many abstaining MPs before an important vote. The Chemistry professor, who had just joined the university and was the youngest of the lot, got the hint from the attitude of his seniors and climbed in to sit in the seat next to Satish with a resigned look on his face.

Satish had been driving a cab long enough not to let complaining passengers bother him. Furthermore, his thoughts were elsewhere. After the last drop in Munirka, he was supposed to pick up a passenger from Vasant Kunj to take to the airport. The man had asked him to come by seven and it was already past five. Clearing the empty plastic bottles wasted precious minutes. Then the professors took forever to figure out who was sitting where. An eternity seemed to pass before everyone was settled and they were ready to go.

No sooner had they started than the Sociology professor told Satish to turn on the AC. Satish had been hoping to keep it off. The AC had the effect of relaxing tired limbs and inducing sleep. Then the English professor instructed him to switch off the radio because he wanted to rest. The blaring radio had played its part in keeping Satish awake. What was more, the others also followed the English professor's lead. Instead of conversing, they leaned back in their seats and closed their eyes, ensuring silence reigned inside the cab.

Somehow, Satish forced his eyes to stay open, willing the jaded Xylo forward as fast as he could. On his mind was the level crossing fifteen minutes from the university. Three trains were due to pass at that hour, which meant the iron gate could drop down to block their path any minute. A ten-minute wait at that gate would push them back by half an hour in Delhi, given the rush-hour traffic. He couldn't afford that with a pickup at seven looming on the horizon.

He jammed down on the accelerator, weaving through traffic, running a red light, overtaking other vehicles by crossing over to the wrong side of the road... When his passengers protested, he said that he was trying to make it before the phatak closed. That shut them up. They were keen to get home after a long day and were well aware of the delay the phatak could cause. None of them said anything even as the road narrowed, once they entered a village, and tenements huddled together to their right and left, and little boys, dressed in shorts and vests, played a variety of games in front of their homes.

The Xylo heaved like a pregnant woman in labour as it clattered in and out of potholes on the winding village road. The professors held on to anything they could find, their anxious eyes scanning the road in front for the phatak. A collective sigh of relief sounded as the phatak was found to be open in the distance. But then the iron gate began to drop and five voices rose in unison to exhort Satish to go faster. He needed no encouragement.

Two little boys, dressed in khaki shorts and white vests, were throwing a tennis ball back and forth next to the road. The one with straight hair combed back from his forehead threw the ball harder than usual so that it shot through the hands of his playmate, who had curly hair and bounced on the cracked road in the direction of the level crossing. Anxious to catch up with it before it reached the phatak, the curly-haired boy took off after it just as the Xylo burst down the road at high speed.

It was over before anyone knew it. A skid followed by shrieking tyres, before the Xylo jerked to a halt. Satish and the professors froze in their seats. The phatak had lost all relevance for them. Thoughts of getting home or making it to the pickup at seven had vanished. They couldn't hear the whistle of the approaching train or even the sound of its bogeys rattling past a little later. The soul-shattering scream of a little boy, turning around to see the cab bearing down on him like a tank eager to mow him down, was resounding all round them at a pitch that crossed out everything else.

Stories Chosen from the #HaveASafeJourney Contest

AN END I DID NOT SEE

Ambalika

In hindsight, I should have shut up. After all, it was an event that had to do with 'ideation' and 'innovation', traditionally the domain of the engineering students from NEHU, the North East Hill University, in Shillong. They gave the ideas, presented the prototypes and won prizes. What was I, a mere first year student of English Literature doing in their midst? I was there, in the NEHU campus, representing my college, St Anthony's, at the debate competition held on the occasion of 'Road Safety Week'.

The speakers, including me, had all said what they had to and were now waiting for the results. At that time, I heard of the 'Safety Ideation Contest' that was to start shortly in the auditorium.

'Is it open to us?' I enquired enthusiastically.

'Since when did Shakespeare start working on electronic circuits?' a particularly rowdy-looking chap sneered. I ignored him. With no prototype or diagram to bolster my idea, I was not going to win anyway. My intention was to talk about the misfortunes brought about by bad habits while driving and what technology should do to prevent those. 'Go on', I was told by Mr Rowdy, obviously one of the organisers, rather condescendingly. 'Let us see what wisdom a literature student can impart.'

'Sirs and madams,' I started pitching my idea right away. I told the panel about the biker I had seen skid off the road, and narrowly miss getting his head crushed under a speeding truck. He had been talking on his mobile. 'And that is why I propose this mobile signal jammer for vehicles.' I concluded my speech after a very rudimentary description of what this device could be like. Mission accomplished, I went back to join my team mates who jubilantly informed me that we had won the debate competition. Later, during the prize-distribution ceremony, I was surprised when I heard my name being called out a second time. I was being awarded a consolation prize for my road safety idea! As I went up to the stage, I could see Mr Rowdy actually smile at me, sheepishly.

But that was not all. One of the panelists, Dr Jeevan Sarmah, a renowned professor of electronics, came up to me and spoke about actually developing my idea.

'But, Sir, I am not qualified,' I protested. I told him of how my knowledge realm did not revolve around protons and electrons. Neither Macbeth nor Miranda from my world could be persuaded to worry about soldering capacitors and resistors onto a circuit board. Dr Sarmah, however, was not going to listen to any of it and before I knew what I had got myself into, I found myself in the drawing room of the Sarmah household.

Sargam Aunty, Dr Sarmah's wife (she insisted that I call her 'Sargam Aunty' and not the conventional 'Ma'am') laughed when he told her how I had come into this project. 'Just like our Vinny, so full of rebellion,' she remarked. I blushed a beetroot red! It was only the tea and freshly fried samosas that helped me return to my usual self.

'Vinny and you will get on like a house on fire!' she said with a mischievous twinkle in her eyes. As she excused herself to pack tiffin for Vinny, I noticed that she had the most affectionate face I had ever seen. For the next one month, her tea, wit and remarks about Vinny, her daughter, became my steady companions as I stumbled about trying to find my way in the world of electronics, sitting in that drawing room. As Dr Sarmah explained the various technical concepts, I could always hear Sargam Aunty in the background complaining about Vinny. 'The girl is never around when I need her!' was a regular grumble, followed by, 'I wish her father did not pamper her so much!'

On hearing this, Dr Sarmah would smile indulgently at first and then frown. Twice, he got up from our study session to pacify her. 'There now, it is settled!' he would say as he returned in good cheer. By the end of the month, I had made significant progress. If I could get my sensors right, I might as well declare myself as an inventor of a good road safety product. But then I went and burned those devices while soldering them.

Though it was quite late in the evening, I was eager to buy new ones and solder them back onto the board. 'If only Vinny had returned by now, she could have come with you,' Sargam Aunty said.

'That would be kind of you and Vinny! Maybe another time,' I said and thanked her.

The next day, I arrived with my freshly soldered board. But in my attempt to get things right, I had got a little delayed and forgotten to inform Dr Sarmah about it. As a result, I found he was not at home. After a few moments of chatting with Sargam Aunty, I said, 'It's become quite dark! Maybe Vinny can drop me back today, Aunty. You think she will?' Taking the public transport in Shillong could be quite stressful at the best of times, what with the congested roads, and at this hour, it was simply not advisable.

'Oh, then you will have to wait the entire night till morning, my dear!' she replied.

'Why?'

'Well, she has gone for that pop concert. Obviously, she will be late!'

'Eh? Which one, Aunty?' No college student likes to

miss a pop concert. I was secretly fuming at myself for having missed this one.

'That funny band... don't really know the name... something to do with a rocking Michael.'

'Michael Learns To Rock!' I said, unable to hold my laughter. But this was news to me. MLTR was in town and I had no clue of it? I mean, seriously? Had I got so absorbed with my circuits that I had totally missed something as significant as an MLTR show? Maybe I was over reacting. Just over a year ago, I had attended their last show.

A light drizzle earlier that evening had thrown in an unexpected romantic charm to the performance held at the Nehru Stadium. But though I remembered it like yesterday, I would still give anything to attend another one of their shows! I felt a little disappointed at having missed the recent one. 'Where is it this time, Aunty?'

'Nehru Stadium,' she replied.

I should have guessed! It was the only location in Shillong fit for a music band of that stature. Wait, I had just walked past the Nehru Stadium a few minutes back. I had not noticed any crowd.

'It is just you and me for tiffin today,' she said, as she laid the tea and snacks on the table. Meanwhile, I quietly Googled the details of the concert. The search results showed that there were none for that day! In fact, no Nehru Stadium in any part of the country was hosting them. So, why did Sargam Aunty lie?

'What time does the concert start, Aunty?' I asked trying not to sound suspicious.

'Seven o'clock,' she replied.

At that moment, Dr Sarmah entered the room. He was understandably surprised to see me. But his surprise soon gave way to anger when he noticed the tea that was laid out on the table. 'What is this, Sargam?' he demanded of his wife. Then, having realised that it was a futile question to ask, he merely walked out of the room. He motioned for me to join him outside the house. Dr Sarmah seemed to have aged in those few minutes. His face was grave. There was no trace of his usual jovial self. 'I hope she has not been telling you about Vinny going to some concert today?'

'Why yes, Sir, she did say so!'

'Of course it is not true,' he added hastily. I said nothing. 'She had gone last year. To Nehru Stadium. It had rained a little that day. She skidded.' Instead of reaching the stadium, she landed at the emergency ward of St Joseph's hospital. Instead of cheering for her superstars, she had turned into a little star, later that night.

Clearly, time had not helped Sargam Aunty move beyond this incident. In her consciousness, Vinny still lived. So she made up her bed, even though it remained unslept in and she put a plate for her on the table during breakfast, lunch and dinner. To her, Vinny's absence was merely one of her pranks to annoy her mother. Nothing more.

'It wasn't the rain that had made Vinny's scooty skid,' Dr Sarmah added. 'She had been talking on her cellphone.' Tears welled up in his eyes. 'I had called her up to check if she had reached. Look where I sent her!'

SAFETY FIRST

Anukriti Verma

'HELLO! I AM THE LITTLE GIRL WHO LIVES BESIDE THE road that you drive past every day. You often perform a variety of stunts which frighten me. No, I am not impressed. My Amma, too, gets scared; she isn't impressed either. I don't think anyone would be. The other day my friend Birju got hurt because of your so-called brave stunts. His mother didn't have enough money to take him to a hospital and you just drove away. We are human too. Treat us like you treat everyone else.'

Sarah clapped loud and hard for Joanna, her eight-year-old daughter, who was acting out this role in the school fancy-dress competition. Sarah felt very proud of her daughter. After reaching home, both Sarah and her husband Martin hugged and appreciated Joanna for her heartwarming performance. For dinner, Sarah had made Joanna's favourite pasta with white sauce and roasted vegetables, but the little girl was so excited with all the attention, she could hardly eat anything. For that matter, neither could Sarah and Martin. But the reason for their unease was different. Joanna's older brother Rick was nowhere to be seen. He should have been home for dinner. He hadn't even called to say he would be late. Ever since that fateful day and the torturous months that followed, Sarah and Martin could not relax until they knew Rick was safe.

They used to try hard to put that memory out of their minds, but they didn't always succeed.

◆

Rick had turned eighteen seven months ago, almost to the day, and he had been gifted his first ever motor bike. Martin and Sarah were reluctant to get him one, but he was so persuasive, promising to be careful and all that, that they had finally agreed. It was a very stylish black beast, with a powerful 150 cc engine. Most of Rick's friends were very jealous of him. They would wheedle him to go for a spin on it, some even begged him to let them ride it themselves! But Rick was possessive of his bike. He spent all day on the road, zooming around aimlessly. This perturbed his parents an awful lot. But Rick being the 'cool kid', turned a deaf ear to their concern. He even snubbed them for being too protective and not letting him grow up. Soon the neighbours complained that his revving the engine and racing around especially in the afternoons and late nights was disturbing them. The college authorities informed his parents that Rick was very irregular and his attendance was falling short. They would have to take action against him. Sometimes Sarah and Martin tried to make him understand with love, at other times with anger. But all in vain. They soon realised that the daily arguments were straining their relationship with him; he hardly spoke to them and would stay away from home for as long as possible. Fearing the growing distance from their son, Sarah and Martin decided to keep quiet and let him have his way.

Little did they know this would be a decision they would regret for years to come.

◆

17 January was a regular day. Joanna had just come back from school and Sarah was getting her lunch ready. Martin was at work. The phone rang. Sarah answered it with a chirpy 'Hello!', just like she always did. But what she heard froze her. Her legs could not support her and she sat down on the chair with a thump. Joanna was puzzled. She realised something was wrong. With trembling hands Sarah dialled Martin's number and asked him to reach City Hospital at once.

Sarah requested her neighbour to look after Joanna for that day and rushed out. Within the next fifteen minutes, she and Martin were standing outside the Intensive Care Unit, startled, looking vacantly at the white walls of the hospital. Rick and his friend, Alex, had met with a terrible accident. Both had been badly injured, their faces could not be recognised. Alex's parents had been informed and were on their way to the hospital. After what seemed like hours, the doctors came up to the distraught parents and broke the devastating news. Rick's condition was critical but Alex was no more.

Rick and Alex had been best friends since primary school. The seed of their friendship had been sown in Class Three when Alex had saved Rick from the bullies of Class Six. Rick on his part used to make sure that Alex never came to class without completing his homework. Over the years, their bond had grown stronger and they were like brothers. Everyone called them the real life Jai and Veeru from *Sholay*. Jai and Veeru? Quite literally. Jai had decided to leave Veeru alone and go further on his eternal journey. Veeru was still unaware of Jai's departure.

'Do not let Rick know of Alex's demise. His condition is critical and any sort of stress should be avoided for him to recover,' the doctors warned.

Alex's parents were stoic in their grief. They never blamed Rick for what happened, they did not make Sarah and Martin feel they were responsible for the loss of their son. On the contrary, they helped Rick's parents see him through those difficult days in the hospital. A couple of months passed and Rick's condition gradually improved. He came out of coma and was able to recognise his family. Soon, he started speaking short sentences. He had no memory whatsoever of the accident. But every now and then he would demand to see Alex. So often would he ask to see his friend that it became impossible for the doctors and his parents to keep the news hidden any longer.

One day, when the doctors gave the nod, Sarah broke the news. Rick turned into a stone. His friend for over a decade was no more. How could this have happened? And this shocking moment triggered the activation of his brain cells that had gone numb since the accident. He was able to recollect the exact sequence of events that led to this humungous loss.

'It was my fault! It was all my fault, Ma!' he exclaimed. 'I am the reason why Alex is no more today! How could I have done this to my own brother?' Rick was shattered. But greater than his grief was the sense of remorse that he would have to live with throughout his life. While Rick's physical condition improved, the family had to deal with his mental state even after the doctors declared him fit to go home. But his sense of guilt crippled him. He was unable to do any work. How could he ever forgive himself for what had happened to his closest companion?

After many counselling sessions, Rick found the answer to make his life worth living again. He went up to his parents one morning and told them what he wanted to do: 'I want to spread awareness on road safety. I want to start a campaign on Facebook, Twitter and Instagram to make sure another Rick does not end up killing another Alex.' Martin and Sarah gave him full support. The campaign was called 'Drive Safe, Your Life's at Stake'.

Rick and his friends put their heart and soul into making the campaign a huge success. Soon, they had been able to succeed in gathering over five hundred volunteers who went around the city in groups of ten, mostly to schools and colleges, talking about road safety. Sarah and Martin did their part by addressing parents in various clubs, asking them to think very hard before entrusting their youngsters' lives to powerful bikes and fast cars so as not to burden themselves with regret and remorse. Even little Joanna contributed her bit through the fancy dress speech she put on.

The success of the campaign attracted the attention of the authorities and they invited Rick to give a talk at the annual Road Safety Week. On stage, Rick narrated his story, pouring his heart out in front of hundreds of children and various dignitaries. Teary-eyed, he dedicated this campaign to his friend, confessing how it was his own devil-may-care attitude that had cost his friend his life. He would give anything to have his friend back. 'But,' he said, 'I want all of you to know and always remember that it *is* cool to wear a helmet. It *is* cool to drive safely. It *is* equally cool to get a license before you drive. It *is* cool to follow traffic rules. But you know what is not cool? Bunking schools to hit the roads with friends, jumping traffic lights and risking your life and that of your loved ones is definitely not cool. So maybe it is time we all joined hands to redefine cool.' He ended by asking the entire hall to raise their arms and take a pledge to drive safe. As he walked down the stage that day, the entire hall broke into thunderous applause while his heart called out to his friend in heaven. One precious life lost, but hundreds saved. As things change, maybe Alex and numerous others like him, who lost their lives on the roads, will finally rest in peace.

THE PERILOUS EVE

Aritri Chatterjee

PRABIR WOKE UP LATE THAT DAY. IT WAS THE 31ST of December, a day of universal celebration, and he was allowed a little lethargy on this particular day. Though he came from a Bengali family, he too observed the tradition of celebrating the Gregorian New Year. Besides, this was the time he was granted a grand two consecutive days of leave by his employer. He looked down as he scratched his protruding belly. The sweat and oil clinging to his body had transferred onto the already discoloured bedsheet. Funny how he perspired so much even in the middle of winter. Prabir's booming voice broke the morning silence. 'Bring my tea,' he ordered. Shanti rushed into the room, as if on cue, with his tea and a plate of rusks bought from the local bakery at the beginning of the month. Prabir threw a disgusted look at the poorly clad woman and snatched the plate from her hands.

Shanti stood in a corner of the room, awaiting further instructions that her husband might choose to give. After some minutes of prolonged silence during which Prabir slurped his tea, Shanti spoke in a timid, indistinct voice. 'There is no sugar in the house for the evening tea... when you go out can you...' She waited for the wrath of her husband because it was only the 31st and Prabir's meagre salary would come only by the 5th of the month.

Prabir flung the empty cup and plate at the wall and strode towards Shanti's trembling body. He held her plaited hair in a tight grip and with his other hand, twisted her arm. How dare she tell me what to do, he thought. 'Do you think I have a stash of black money at my disposal? Why is it that all the necessities in the kitchen get depleted at your touch? My mother never complained to my dad about the groceries. You are so inauspicious for this household.' The frustration caused from a near-empty wallet found release in the form of physical violence on his wife. Shanti twisted and shrank into herself, pleading with him to let her go. Prabir released his grip and shoved her against the wall. Two distinctive stains adorned the wall now—a brown one from the thrown tea, and the other fresh from the cut on Shanti's forehead.

◆

Shiv crept into the vacant room adjacent to the living area. Myriad sounds seeped in from the party his parents were hosting for their friends. He needed to get away from it. He opened the third drawer of the desk where his father kept all his important documents. Shiv was confident that this is where the keys to his new bike were securely stored. If it wasn't for his mother's nagging, his father would not have taken the keys back from him. Except for the minor accident a week back, Shiv had a completely clean record. He took pride in his riding skills and was considered a champion among his friends. But his mother worried about the scratch on his knee and declared that she could foresee numerous such accidents taking place in the future if Shiv had his way with the motorcycle. Shiv barely needed to search for the keys. He grabbed them and stealthily crept out the back door of his two-storeyed house. A quick call to Deep and the New Year eve no longer seemed boring.

◆

Shanti heard her husband making some appointments for later that evening. She knew what that meant. Her husband would return home stone drunk in the middle of the night. This was not at all unusual as he spent most of his evenings with people she hardly knew. But the previous day he had promised their son that they would watch the New Year's eve celebration on television together. Shanti was torn between the prospects of reminding him and facing his wrath and making a lame excuse to the six-year-old boy. Prabir came out of the bedroom in a grey shirt and a pair of hastily ironed cotton pants. Shanti took small steps towards her husband and attempted a civilised conversation. Prabir was unnecessarily rude and walked out hurling abuses at her.

◆

Shiv had also picked up a bottle of Johnny Walker from his father's cabinet before leaving the house. The noise and commotion was killing him and only a ride in the deserted night could calm his nerves. He took a swift right turn into the dingy lane that led to the gate of Deep's little house. Deep's grandmother was fast asleep when he came out with a windcheater and two woollen scarves in his hands. He handed one to Shiv and hopped onto the pillion seat. Shiv was glad that Deep only had a handful of friends, otherwise he, too, would have been partying the night away. Prior to this, Shiv had declined his friends' invitations since his parents wanted him to be present at their party.

At Deep's suggestion, they stopped at a secluded spot, away from the regular patrol areas of police cars and guaranteed to be out of the radar of local goons and thieves. Deep had had his fair share of experiences in the past to have acquainted himself with such shady details. As soon as they pulled up by the side of the road, Shiv took out the bottle and took a giant swig. He passed the bottle to his friend, whose eyes bulged at the sight of the expensive liquor. His greed got the better of him and he took hasty gulps, fearing that Shiv might change his mind about sharing the whisky. Before long, the bottle was empty. Deep then took out the roll of weed he had procured for his friend—his way of showing his resourcefulness. It was a little before the clock struck twelve when Shiv, the slightly less intoxicated one, hopped onto the bike, with Deep sitting behind him. He drove through the almost deserted road at a decent speed, before the alcohol made its presence felt to the rapidly dulling brain, and the adrenaline kicked in. He accelerated, and the high he got from the speed felt insanely good. Deep was thoroughly enjoying this night; he felt as though he were in paradise. The strong breeze seemed to numb his senses.

The impact took place in a matter of seconds. Even though Shiv had automatically swerved his bike, it took several more seconds for the incident to register in his mind. Then he saw the damaged body lying on the sidewalk and the splatter of what seemed to be the brains of the man who lay dead. The black SUV had rushed away into the darkness.

Shiv had slowed down, both by the physical as well as the psychological impact of the accident. He tried to make a turn to check if the man was still alive. Deep's strong and cautious hand held his shoulders tightly. 'Don't,' he said, trying to persuade Shiv as much as himself that they couldn't be of any help. He urged Shiv to drive quickly away from the scene. The blood- and dirt-stained grey shirt and cotton pants lay in the middle of the lonesome road.

◆

Shanti kept checking the clock desperately. Beads of sweat had gathered on her forehead and upper lip. Her little son slept peacefully in the inner room after bouts of tears and lame excuses and consolations. His father had not kept his word. His evening enjoyment had extended late into the night. Shanti could hear the sound of fireworks that marked the beginning of another tiresome year for her. She had almost fallen asleep when the shrill ringing of the telephone next to the cupboard startled her. She quickly picked up the receiver, her eyes darting to the tiny clock on the table. It was well past 3 a.m. and the phone call could only mean bad news. Her hands shook terribly as she uttered a feeble hello. The voice on the other side of the receiver barely registered in her mind.

THE STREET PHOTOGRAPHER

Arvind Passey

THE DISTRAUGHT INSPECTOR LOOKED UP AND SAID, 'You're late. As usual. Pruthi, life in this thana is not just about your daily beat.'

'I know, Sir,' replied Pandit Ram Murti Pruthi, the constable who stood in slack attention and pondered: 'Why are thana in-charges always so stressed out? He doesn't want to go home even on weekends. But I am married...'

'Now will you stop making a martyr of yourself, Pruthi, and just tell me if you saw anything unusual anywhere?'

'Desi is dead,' said Pruthi, still standing as slack as slack could be defined. He did not yet have a tea belly like almost everyone else in the thana, but his muscles weren't taut enough. The men around him were forever slurping tea and he was convinced that their bellies had started looking like those cheap mugs that had their base bulging out to carry more.

The inspector closed the file that lay in front of him and addressed the two sub-inspectors sitting across the table, 'He comes in late. He comes in to tell me there is a dead man out there in the streets.' Then turning towards Pruthi, he said, 'You know I have five VIP duties to allot today? But with a dead man lying in your beat, how can this be done? Now stop standing there like a scarecrow and tell me what happened.'

Pruthi relaxed his already slack body, breathed in something that filled his head with a syrupy, sticky concoction of air, cigarette smoke, stale dregs of tea from a dozen cups on the floor, and began: 'I was on the other side of the road questioning the owner about the theft in his watch-repair shop when I happened to look up. I saw a hand pushing a fat man...'

The inspector laughed, 'You should go to Mumbai and write for films, Pruthi. You saw a hand in the air? A hand in the air pushing a fat man? Then this fat man falls and his head strikes a pole and by the time you reached him, he was dead? Am I right?'

'Yes, Sir.'

The others in the room clapped in amusement and Kewal Singh, a sub-inspector, quipped, 'You have such an incisive insight into crime, Sir. Arrey, Pruthi, learn from Sir ji.'

'Yes, Sir.'

'Now you may tell your side of the story, Constable Pruthi,' the inspector said, rolling his eyes, a smirk playing on the face. This is the expression most bosses display when their juniors are sitting around and latching on to every word they utter as if the words were the Gangajal of authority. 'And, Pruthi, for promotion's sake, please tuck in your shirt properly. You look like a... chalo, forget it, report your story now.'

'Ji, Sir.' And then Pruthi began to tell the story to no one in particular. 'The traffic was moving on both sides. This seemed normal because this is what I see every day. But it is not easy to cross the road when you need to look left to right and then right to left, Sir. It makes even walking difficult.' The inspector sighed audibly. The room had silence swaying from here to there, mirroring what Pruthi had tried to do before he could get to the other side where a scuffle was taking place.

'This is a traffic problem, Pruthi, not ours,' said the inspector impatiently.

'Yes, Sir.' Pruthi was silent for a while as he thought, *how can reporting be complete if it is not complete?* And then he cleared his throat and began, 'The traffic police were not there. So I used my whistle to stop these defaulters on that road and ran across.' Pruthi paused before adding, 'I have often seen people driving on the wrong side at this point.'

'Thank god you reached somewhere on time,' laughed one of the junior officers in the room.

'No, Sir. I was late,' said Pruthi, 'I was probably late.'

'Decide if you were late or probably late,' said the inspector.

'Definitely late, Sir. Because as I crossed to the other

side I could see the hand clearly. Five rings on five fingers, with the one on the middle finger having a large blue stone...'

'You know what your problem is, Pruthi?' said the inspector, 'You notice everything except what is important. Did it occur to you that the face is what identifies a person fastest?'

'Yes, Sir,' replied Pruthi, 'But before I could reach there, the windows of the car were rolled up. They had dark tinted glasses. I wondered why the traffic police had never caught this fellow. Anyhow, he started his car, ran over the fallen man, turned right when the light was red and disappeared even before I reached the spot on the footpath.'

'Now where did this footpath appear from?'

'He was driving on the footpath, Sir,' said Pruthi. 'So were autos and scooters and motorcycles. I had a terrible time stopping them all and preventing them from running over this man who was already down and bleeding.'

Pruthi remembered how he had bent down, felt the pulse, and known the man was dead. 'He could have died because of his head hitting the pole. Or because the car ran over him,' he muttered, 'There was this camera lying next to him.' Pruthi placed an expensive-looking camera on the table.

The inspector examined the camera and announced, 'Nikon. Digital camera. Expensive. Can this be the case of a rich man stalked and killed? I'm sure it isn't a simple hit-and-run. What do you say?' The inspector looked around but it was obvious that more clues were needed before anyone could volunteer an answer.

'Go on, Pruthi. But hurry. Remember, there is a VIP duty waiting for you.'

'Yes, Sir. I also found a card that says "Desi". And there is some website given and some strange rank written. Street photographer, it says.' Pruthi placed the visiting card on the table. 'I had the dead body shifted to the mortuary, Sir.'

'Investigation is like a big road with lots of signs, Pruthi,' said the inspector, 'And lots of traffic going both here and there. But let us first see if this camera tells a tale.' They browsed through the final lot of photographs of traffic rules being blatantly violated. Haywire traffic resembling the tangle of electricity cables that everyone sees everywhere. Pictures of pedestrians with pained looks of shock at discovering a speeding truck on the footpath. Cycles and scooters jammed head-to-head, which is quite unlike the conventional tail-to-tail jamming, resembled a collision just before it actually happens. There was even one shot where an old woman was walking precariously on the uneven boundary wall that separated the footpath from a construction site.

'I am out on this road so often,' said the inspector, 'but I never thought things were so bad. I guess Desi was doing his job as a street photographer rather well.'

'Yes, Sir,' said Pruthi out of sheer habit.

And then there was the picture of a car with one hand of the driver out of the window, fiddling with a sticker on the windshield. 'The hand, Sir,' shouted Pruthi, 'this is the car.' But the shot was probably attempted when the car must have been near and so the registration number wasn't visible. The occupants were not visible. Dark tints to blame, of course. All that was visible was the hand with rings on all fingers, a ring with a large blue stone on the middle finger.

'You have a keen observation, Pruthi,' said the inspector, 'and you will go far. But now that the car has disappeared and Desi is already dead, let us forget them for a while. You need to go to Imperial cinema in Chuna Mandi and relieve sub-inspector Dinesh who is on VIP duty for Shubh Kaamji. He is the son of our minister for law and order. Shadow him. Follow him. Make sure he is not troubled by pranksters.'

With a final 'Yes, Sir', Pruthi turned and walked out of the station.

'Good that you're here, Pruthi,' said Dinesh as Pruthi stood inside Imperial cinema feeling a bit lost. 'Come, let me introduce you... Shubh Sir, Pruthi is an intelligence officer and will be with you. Now I will take your leave.' Dinesh saluted the minister's son smartly and went out. Pruthi smiled and stood watching his VIP talk to the businessmen of the area. And then his eyes noticed Shubh Kaam's right hand, the rings, and the middle finger with a large blue stone.

Pruthi discretely stepped a few steps away and called the thana in-charge, 'Sir, I have traced the hand in the Desi murder case. It is Shubh Kaam.'

'Good,' said the inspector, 'Now just do your duty properly.' Disconnecting the call, the inspector called Shubh Kaam's father, the minister, and said, 'Sir, I have something very important to show. Need to meet you immediately.'

Two days later, Pruthi was informed that his dedication towards his duty was being rewarded and he was, therefore, transferred to a thana near his home in outer Delhi. The Desi murder case file, some believe, is with the minister and he uses it to fan himself whenever he feels low.

MISPLACED DREAMS

Barnali Ray Shukla

THE MOUNTAINS LOOKED TALLER AND MORE GUARDED in an ominous silence baring only little. The conifers nodded in anticipation as if they knew a secret message… a message which would remain in the folds of the mountains forever.

CHASING A PIECE OF CLOUD was another post for my blog by the very same name.

I found a different me in this post. Impressions of a silent drive in that bus towards Aru Valley from Srinagar, Kashmir, last July. We were all heading to Baaltaal, the Amarnath base camp. Umesh was snoring on my left. Tanmay on my right, was singing softly to himself as he stared out of the window. His nostrils flared slightly on the lower notes of the song. A faded sticker of Bollywood icon Shah Rukh Khan with a bleeding heart and arrow reminded us of demi-gods, and the indigo kitschy painting of Lord Shiva on the ceiling of the bus was a reminder of gods watching over us. We were on seat numbers 23,

25, 27 in a blue and white bus, 3 X 3 seating, non AC.

Tanmay stretched out his left palm, still staring out of the window. I understood his need for nicotine. And extended a bar of Kit-Kat. He cursed me under his breath, looked at me and then at the iPad screen, read for exactly 90 seconds and deleted my blog post.

I pushed his face against the dusty glass in a merciless grip. He didn't yelp in pain, I did. 'That was work, dammit!'

'You call that topographical masturbation work?'

'Who the hell lets you decide that, you moron?' I almost throttled Tanmay. He managed to turn around and threatening to delete an earlier blog, snatched the packet of cigarettes from my jacket. Umesh broke into a trashy Bollywood song, singing at the top of his voice. The co-passengers were too tired to protest. But the driver cheered, and offered to halt at the spot where this particular song had been shot. He pulled over. I hurled Umesh out of the bus. There was a ripple of grateful murmur. The driver took out a hip flask. This evoked a mixed response from the passengers. The assistant announced that it was just a potion. It came with a doctor's prescription. The potion must have been potent, the driver fell silent. The passengers fell silent too.

This journey, on JK-015-0941, had started a few hours earlier with 43 passengers, 21 men, 12 women, 8 children, the driver and his assistant. A journey of 126 kilometres at an altitude of 4311 metres above sea level. The smoke from sickly sweet incense swirled to tingle our noses. A bright yellow plastic hibiscus garland was parked at the feet of the ceramic idol of Lord Shiva. Remixed songs in praise of Lord Shiva offered a shade of comfort as they played on a rickety cassette player. The women sang along with closed eyes, men burped, children cried, young adults got restless. How much longer, asked a male voice. The driver didn't reply, the assistant was lost in an MMS clip.

The setting sun had painted the sky a deep magenta smeared with shades of orange. I don't remember the last time I had looked the sun in the eye. Then it was suddenly very dark. The hair-pin bends in the road promised light at some of the darkest turns as this was a two-way road. At the last hair-pin bend, the headlights chased away the darkness. There was no gasp of wonder this time. Instead, a deathly silence. The bus had left the road and was heading towards the gorge, in a near nose dive. Three wheels must have been in mid air by now. The driver had fallen asleep.

My eyes turned to Tanmay Tuli, a dentist in the business of fixing smiles. He had it all perfect. A successful career, one wife, one child, one dog, one set of happy parents, one rich brother in the Gulf, one married and now pregnant sister in the USA on Skype. Each year they went for two vacations, two weddings and one funeral. He, Umesh and I had been classmates at the medical entrance coaching class, trying to live up to our parents' expectations of becoming surgeons. None of us made it finally.

Umesh Bansal was the manager of the swanky Nehru

Place branch of State Bank of India. His father had been missing since the 1984 riots. His mother had raised him all by herself. Her quest had always been to find her husband. She was still hopeful that he would return. Umesh was sure his father was dead, but he supported his mother in her efforts to find him. However, last April when his mother almost brought home a mummy and declared it was her lost husband, Umesh knew he had to bring closure to the matter. He had planned to call his mother and tell her that they had found her husband's frozen and perfectly poised handsome body near the Amarnath shrine. Umesh's dislike for children ensured that he never married. But he was obsessed with women. His receding hairline, pompous attitude and pan-stained teeth made him repulsive to them, but he wasn't asking for their acceptance. When he needed a lay, he found one.

They call me KD. Krishnakant Deshpande. Born into a family of celebrated and decorated doctors. I sat for the medical entrance examination. Except for my self-esteem and the calendar, nothing suffered.

My life had not been a stable one. I had changed 23 jobs in 15 years. I was not sure about anything. Except Sapna, my ophthalmologist friend. Despite the dash of salt in her hair, she was still a dream girl. She had given eyesight to over 187 people and was herself the cynosure of all eyes. I was planning to move in with her before I became a relic. My friends were sure she would dump me, but I was confident we would stay together because of our mutual dread of the 'M' word—marriage. Sapna's dream was to spend more and more time working in villages, conducting eye camps. And I was determined to make her dream a reality, no matter what it took.

I was going on the Amarnath pilgrimage, neither to pray nor to thank God, but to ask for forgiveness! Of all the people I wanted to say sorry to, I think my father's face came first to my mind. Maybe because I don't think I ever liked him. I felt he had let me down. I, in turn, did the same. I wanted to tell my father that I will change. I wanted to tell him that his son would be a better man from the next day. I typed a message on my phone: 'THANK YOU VERY MUCH FOR YOUR CONCERN, YOU ARE PROBABLY RECEIVING YOUR LAST SMS FROM THIS PERSON'. Seconds later, I pressed 'send'.

Minutes passed, rolled into an hour and now almost two... there was no response. My mother didn't call either. I must have been unwanted from the day I was born. I sounded like a total loser to my own ears. I wanted to believe that my father hadn't received the message. I sent the same sms to Tanmay and Umesh. Their respective phones beeped, they read it almost instantly. Tanmay gave me a condescending snigger and showed his middle finger under my nose. Umesh slapped me, 'And why would you send this message? Suicide attempt or you want to test us?' That's when I realised the impact my message could have. They all thought this was my last message to them. I never thought of the consequences this could have on my life. Or my forthcoming death!

This was my way to announce that I couldn't continue to be the person I was becoming. They read the SMS, they didn't get the message.

Last week, I had stolen. I had stolen lots of money, in cash, from my office. No one understood and now inches away from perishing in this birth, I wonder if they ever will. The bus tumbled further. The music player, which had stopped, resumed playing as if on cue.

I was telling myself this was one of my nightmares and I was soon going to wake up. But this was a nightmare of the real kind, where mortality hits you between the eyes and skulls opened up like melons. Damn! Why didn't I get my car? And all that cash that I had stolen! How would it reach Sapna?

I knew I could help Sapna with her dream, someone had to. She wanted the blind to see and the deaf to hear and the mute to find a voice. I told her one evening, 'When the blind would see... they would also hear.' She had smiled suspiciously, though I know she wanted to step onto the edge of hope. Moments later, her logical mind threw up a question to the romantic in me. I had to explain that I wasn't merely trying to be like a lighthouse in a stormy sea. She still refused to see the logic. I attempted again. 'I read lips.' Sapna was listening. I continued: 'If I can read lips with my eyes, I can listen even if I can't hear.' She half nodded. 'So, the new-found eyes, one day, will hear too.' Sapna looked amused.

'Hence proven that when the blind will be able to see, they will soon learn to *hear*.' She completed the sentence. 'And one day they would find a voice too.' Sapna had looked at me for what felt like eternity. Had we just redefined the five senses all over again? Touch and smell were the only two senses that weren't brought up that evening. I had felt an aching need to make love to her under the sky, that very instant. Before my lips could complete the prayer, she got up and left, without a word, some bits of grass still fresh on her loose plait. She had taken the next morning train to the same village. 'Life is too short,' she would say when I used to sit by myself and sulk. 'Go and do things which you always meant to.' I chose to go on a pilgrimage.

I looked down. The bus had turned turtle completely and was almost into the deep gorge. Umesh held on to my wrist and screamed to the lord to let him live. He wanted to say sorry to someone. Tanmay was the one who usually never got ruffled, but right now his legs were caught between seats 25 and 27. And all he could think of was screaming out his daughter's name. My phone started ringing somewhere. Ma calling! I wanted to pick up the phone, but it slipped away, out of my reach and left me forever.

The last time Sapna was in Delhi she had asked me if all was okay. I had lied. One day, she left.

She had said: 'When your smile reaches your eyes like it used to... I will come back.'

The bus now was cracking into something hot and flaming. Tanmay was trying to smile. 'You think Neena will marry again?' he whispered.

Umesh didn't find this funny; he was desperately yelling into his phone. He was telling some man that he should take his mother to DCP Pathak at Daryaganj PS. Also to remind her of her visa interview as now it would be better if she visits her sister in Singapore next week. Umesh screamed on the phone asking the man at the other end of the line to delete all the MMSs from his desktop, said that the password was Sunny Leone. Umesh's neck snapped before he could give the next instruction.

I tried to picture what was happening to my parents at this point of time. I had let them down. My best was yet to come. I was still alive but had lost count of time. I threw away all my parameters to count, weigh, gauge. That's the real journey, the travel of a lifetime. I think what I first lost today was my voice. And then I lost Tanmay to flames. And then I lost my hearing. But I could still see. I could read lips. And all I could read when I looked at the various lips around me was the love for life—prayers for loved ones and confessions which should have been made long back, regrets that had replaced dreams. I wasn't falling, I wasn't. I seemed to be escaping into the mysterious world of clouds and conifers to hear what their last secret was... blogs could be deleted from iPads but memories remained forever. I felt nothing. It was all bright.

HOW BRIEF WAS YOUR STAY

Dipali Taneja

My darling Chanda, it's just a matter of weeks now when both of us get big 'promotions'—you become a mother, and I become a brand new grandmother. I'm excited, and happy, and oh-so-nervous. I know that you have had a reasonably smooth pregnancy—no complications, you've been exercising, walking, and eating healthy, and you have a wonderful doctor too. And yet, the birth of each and every child is, to me, always a miracle. And your first baby will be your own personal miracle...

Your father and I will be with you soon. God bless you, Chanda. Love to Vivek.
Yours, Ma

I will not upset my pregnant daughter with the story of the tragic loss of my first baby. And yet, her impending delivery brings back so many memories...

Twenty-nine years later, I still mourn my first-born daughter. Had things been different, she would have been here still, on this planet of ours, perhaps a mother herself...

My beloved little Tara, I am still bereft. God has been very kind to us, you have a younger brother and a sister, and your sister will soon deliver her first child. They are still deciding what to name her. You would have, I imagine, been the proudest maasi ever, a fond aunt happily guiding her sister on all matters related to babies!

While I was expecting you, I had all kinds of fears. I was scared of miscarrying, scared of birth defects, scared of dropping you, scared of infections... A friend had lost her newborn son to SIDS, cot death, something totally inexplicable and tragic. It took Rahul, your papa, huge efforts to comfort me and reassure me that it wouldn't happen to our baby. And yet, despite all these misgivings, I made a conscious effort to remain happy and cheerful throughout my pregnancy. The tremendous love I felt for you, this tiny person growing in my womb, helped me overcome my fears and look forward to your arrival. Your nana and nani came and stayed with us. Nani was indulgent and pampering as never before. She cooked my favourite dishes, massaged my swollen feet, and told me all kinds of stories about me as a little girl, while your nana took me on long walks, morning and evening, to make sure that I would be strong and fit to deliver my precious baby, their first grandchild. Rahul would try and come home early from office; he would drive us all down to Hazratgunj where I would enjoy my favourite matar chaat.

Those were beautiful days, full of happiness and the promise of joys yet to come. I would forget about the sleepless nights and the constant pressure on my bladder, and bask in the glow of love that surrounded me.

Your dada and dadi were away in the USA, where your cousin Sona, your Seema Bua's baby, had just arrived. They planned to be back before your third-month birthday. They would phone once in a while, make sure that Rahul was looking after me properly, and were most relieved to know that my mother would stay on for the first forty days post-delivery. My papa planned to go back to Bangalore once we were back from the hospital and more or less settled into a routine. Perhaps it was thanks to those walks and all the care I received that I had a very smooth and uneventful delivery.

You, my dear little Tara, arrived in this world weighing seven pounds and five ounces, and were tall at twenty-two inches. We went through several sleepless nights together, you and I, as we tried to establish a breastfeeding routine. You learned to latch on, but would soon fall asleep and stop nursing, only to wake up within half an hour because you were hungry again!

Burping, changing, bathing, massaging, Nani did all that she could to help, alongside training the ayah we had employed, who was with us from morning to evening. And then it was time for Nani to leave.

You were six weeks old. Dada and Dadi would be coming home in another few weeks. Seema Bua had bought lots of stuff to send with them. Both Seema and I had some great conversations over the phone—two young mothers exchanging notes about their first-born babies. Bua told me how infant car seats were mandatory in the US, and how she really wanted to send one for Baby Tara, but your dada and dadi had laughed, and told her that we didn't even have seat belts in our cars, so a car seat would be quite pointless! Bua agreed; she hadn't been in the US for so long that she'd forgotten Indian realities, but said that in that case it made even greater sense to always sit in the rear seat with the infant. Wise words which were soon forgotten, until that fateful day...

If only I could erase the date from my mind, Tara, of the day you left us forever. It is indelibly etched in my mind. You were exactly eighty-three days old. You had had your DPT vaccine as scheduled, and had recovered from the resultant mild fever. You were cranky with colic most evenings, so your papa and I had to take turns walking with you in an upright position after the ayah had left for the day.

That Saturday evening, we decided to go for a long drive; you usually fell asleep with the movement of the car. We thought we'd go to the cantonment, where the roads were good and less crowded. We had barely crossed Sikandar Bagh when a boy on a bicycle darted in front of the car. Rahul braked hard and swerved and we crashed into the kerb. You were in my arms, Tara, and I instinctively clutched you tight, but not tight enough to prevent your head from hitting the glove compartment. I blacked out, too, as my head hit the windscreen. Rahul was unhurt, fortunately, and neither was the wretched boy on the bicycle; he rode on, unaware of the damage he had caused...

Rahul managed to drive us to the nearest hospital. I had had a severe concussion, and had fractured my elbow with the impact. You, my Tara, my tiny little star, had a swelling in the brain, and died before I regained consciousness.

Your poor father had the unenviable task of calling our families and telling them of this tragedy. Dada and Dadi were leaving the US in a couple of days anyway: it would have been pointless for them to change their flight tickets. They grieved and mourned there with Seema Bua, and were strong and composed when they finally got home to us. Poor Rahul had to bury you without me by his side.

I was terribly weak and still in shock, and had to undergo a surgery to fix my broken elbow. Nana and Nani managed to get here before I was discharged from the hospital. They seemed to have aged overnight. Somehow, though, we all survived, and learned how to live without you.

My heart ached for your dada and dadi, who never got the opportunity of even seeing you or holding you.

But both of them became our pillars of strength. After my elbow had healed and I was able to function, Dadi talked Rahul and me through our fears, and convinced us to have another baby. It was no easy task, as both of us were struggling with painful feelings of guilt and inadequacy.

Why had I forgotten Seema's wise words? Why didn't I sit in the back seat with you, Tara? Would God even trust us with another baby? Dadi persevered, and I am so very glad that she did; thanks to her persistence, our lives are blessed with your brother Suraj, and your sister Chanda. (Yes, we like our children's names to light up the sky.) It has not been easy for them, growing up with parents who are extremely paranoid about their safety. I have also often embarrassed them by insisting that no young child I know is ever allowed to sit in the front seat of a car, until they are old enough and big enough for the seatbelt to provide adequate support. I've spread awareness on this issue in their schools, in our own neighbourhood, and even in Rahul's office.

You live on in 'The Tara Foundation', which works to improve driver and passenger safety in all motor vehicles, including school buses. We keep trying to upgrade our campaign, and emphasise these points: Indian cars now have seat belts both in the front and the back. We need to make the use of rear seatbelts mandatory. It should also be mandatory for infants to ride in safe infant carriers. We keep telling parents that if they can afford to buy a car, they must buy a car seat too, for their infant. And just in case their baby has to ride without a car seat, the precious life should be made to sit safely in the back seat, accompanied by a responsible and alert adult. We keep stressing on never allowing children to jump about in a moving vehicle, or scream or fight… or any activities that can distract the driver. Nor should they ever be allowed to stick their hands and arms or any other body part out of the car windows.

It takes just a momentary lapse of concentration for tragedy to strike.

My dearest, most precious Tara, perhaps you came into our lives for those eighty-three memorable days for a mission: to teach us to help several other parents keep their babies safe while on the road. God bless you.

Gift tag on infant car seat:

Dearest Chanda and Vivek,
Wishing you and our lovely granddaughter many happy and safe rides together!
God bless you all.
With love,
Ma and Papa

A HELPING HAND

Geetanjali Maria

THE TRAFFIC LIGHT CHANGED FROM AMBER TO RED. I cursed the cars in front of me for driving slowly and making me miss the green light. The queue was long and I was impatiently drumming on the steering wheel, thinking about the day's events. It had been a happy day at office. I had received the quarterly award of appreciation for all the efforts that I had put in for my client. Where should I take my family for dinner, I was thinking. Should it be Barbeque Nation or the Radisson Blue, I wondered, when I heard a loud screech, followed by lots of noises—somebody screaming, people calling out, a series of *'aaarghhhs'* and *'oooops'*. Must be an accident.

That's what happens when you day dream or talk on the mobile phone while you drive, I said to no one in particular.

The traffic light turned green and the vehicles started moving. Ahead, to the right, a crowd had gathered. Probably the accident site. I tend to get nauseated by the sight of blood, so I turned away. But somewhere Murphy's Law seemed to be working. The mob carrying the injured person came right in front of my car. They banged on the glass, shouting, asking me to take the person to the hospital. I sat there frozen for a moment, not knowing what to do. All thoughts of the happy moments that I had been enjoying a few seconds ago were erased. Even before I could react, somebody had opened the back door and was getting the injured person in. *Oh shit*! I had forgotten to lock the doors. Now there was no escape. I tried to protest, explain, plead that I couldn't stand the sight of blood. But nobody paid any attention to me in all the commotion and confusion. A couple of other men also got into the back and front seats and asked me to drive quickly to the hospital.

Left with no choice, I obliged. I tilted the rear-view mirror a little higher so that I wouldn't have to see the gory sight in the back. I drove as fast I could to KMP hospital, which was some three kilometres away. The helpers jumped out and carried the injured man into the hospital, muttering a hurried thanks to me. I sat looking straight ahead, white in the face. In my eight years of driving this was the first time I had rushed somebody to a hospital. My brain seemed to have stopped functioning and I was on autopilot. My heart was pounding and I was feeling cold. The shrill whistle of the guard shook me out of my stupor. He asked me to move my car away from the main entrance. I wondered whether I should go in once and check if the person was fine. But the fact that my family was waiting at home for me made me dismiss the thought and I drove away. Once again images of a grand dinner and a beautiful evening began to creep into my head. Only they were spattered with blood.

I turned cautiously to look at the back seat. Just as I feared. It was blood-stained and dirty. I would have to clean it if I wanted to drive to work tomorrow. As for the evening dinner, we'd probably have to take my husband Rahul's car.

It took me another twenty minutes to reach home. I was praying all along that no accident party jumps my way again. My husband was already home by the time I reached. The kids had not come back from their football and guitar classes. As soon as he saw my pale face, he asked, 'What happened? You look washed out.'

I narrated the whole story to him. About how unlucky I was to have got stuck at the red light and how by Murphy's Law I was chosen to take the person to the hospital. He looked at the inside of my white Swift Dzire and remarked, 'This needs a lot of cleaning.'

'Yup,' I replied. 'I'll wash it after I have a cup of coffee.'

'Did Rohan call from his football class?' I asked. Rohan is our younger son, aged nine, studying in the third standard.

'No. Neither has Rohit,' he replied.

'Oh damn! In between all this confusion I forgot to mention that I received the quarterly award today. The only one to receive it in the whole Asia Pacific region,' I said rather dismissively, trying to hide my delight.

'Congrats!' he beamed, squeezing my hands. 'Let's celebrate!'

I had a quick cup of coffee and set about cleaning the car. 'Better to spray it with water now before it dries and the stains get into the fabric,' I said to my husband.

'I can drop the car off at the garage tomorrow evening, they will clean it for you,' he replied.

But I didn't want to wait. I opened the tap and using the hose pipe, watered the seat and the car floor. Blood and mud splashed on to my face, making me cringe. I continued to spray water for a whole five minutes. I had managed to get most of the dirt and stains out. The rest would have to be done by the garage. I left the doors open to let the inside area dry and went in to change into a new evening dress. I was about to step into the bathroom when I heard the phone ring. I waited a few seconds to see if Rahul would pick it up. After several rings he did. I could hear his voice go hoarse and wondered what it was.

'Rhea... Rhea...' he stammered as he came into the bedroom where I was standing, undecided whether to go back into the bathroom or wait to hear him.

'Rhea... umm... it was Deepak, Rohan's friend. He said that Rohan met with an accident and is in the hospital. KMP. We need to go fast.'

'Did you say KMP?'

'Yes, Rhea. He's in KMP.'

I froze. My legs buckled and I collapsed onto the bed. My heart raced. Was it him that I had taken to the hospital? Was it him that I had cursed and grumbled about?

'What is it, Rhea? Don't worry. He'll be fine,' Rahul took my hand as he tried to console me.

'Rahul... Rahul... I'm scared. The person who I dropped at the hospital seemed serious. Could that be our Rohan?'

'No, that wouldn't be him. Don't worry. Get ready, quick!' But I could sense the panic in his voice. Rahul changed quickly into a pair of jeans. I put on the first top that came to hand and rushed out. My lips were constantly moving in prayer. With every heartbeat I was muttering apologies... repenting my reluctance to help. We reached the hospital in ten minutes. After brief enquiries at the reception about a boy involved in an accident case, we rushed to the casualty area where they said that the boy had been sent to the operation theatre for emergency surgery. We waited outside for a good ten minutes before we could find somebody who could tell us what was going on.

As a nurse came out, we immediately bombarded her with questions, 'How is he? Will he be okay? What happened?'

She asked us who we were and then told us that the surgery was going on and would take more time before something definite could be said.

We waited outside, praying. After what seemed an eternity the doctor came out. The expression on his face and on that of his assistants told us that everything had gone okay. We requested to be allowed to go and see him but they asked us to wait for some more time till he was moved to the post-operative/recovery room. We sat outside the operation theatre, warm relief slowly spreading from the nerves in the brain to the fingertips and toes. There were prayers of thanks in our hearts.

'Mummy! Daddy!' We turned around to look at the landing. There stood our little gem, his uniform soiled with dirt and patches of dried blood.

'Mummy! When did you guys come? I saw our car in the car park and knew that you and Dad would be here.'

'But, Rohan, you are okay? You're not hurt? Your friend called us—'

'Sid, Siddharth from my team was hit by a car when we were cycling back home. No one offered to help and take him to the hospital. In fact, people were refusing even when we pleaded. And then when one car came by, some people forced the driver to take him to the hospital. I heard them say something about KMP hospital, so I came here. Why don't people help those who get hurt on the road? How is he now? Is he okay?'

I looked at him in a daze. And hugged him close. He did not know, and I was not about to tell him that I was that reluctant driver. At that moment, I resolved never to turn away from an accident. Help the victim. Who knows who it might be!

A MOMENT OF THRILL

Ketaki Patwardhan

It was 2 June 2016, Jay's birthday. Birthdays had always meant so much to him. But today, his special day was just like any other day. He had to go to college, attend classes, come home. Nothing new, nothing fun. Jay's mom always made his favourite vanilla pudding every year for his birthday. But this time, he couldn't even feel the craving for the pudding. All he wanted to do was drive their new car. He wanted to race it along the expressway. He wanted to feel the adrenaline rush, the thrill that came with driving fast. Just like Alekh, his friend, did with his dad's car. And what was wrong in that? He was turning sixteen this year!

'So what do you want for this birthday?' Jay's dad asked from behind the newspaper, as Jay joined him at the dining table for breakfast. Jay did not reply. He concentrated on his breakfast.

'Your vanilla pudding will be ready when you get back from college,' his mom chimed in. Jay still said nothing.

'What's the matter?' His dad finally noticed his sullen expression.

'I want to drive our car,' mumbled Jay, still looking down at the piece of toast lying on his plate.

'You will drive our car when you are eighteen and have a valid license. We have discussed this before and I don't want to say it again. No more arguments,' his dad said firmly.

'But why? Why can't I when Alekh can?' Jay shouted, his face flushed with anger.

'Because he is a pampered boy of rich parents,' his father yelled back.

Jay pushed away his plate and stood up. 'Wait, Jay, we can talk about this. Don't vent your anger on food,' his mom tried to stop him.

'I hate birthdays!' Jay declared as he stormed out of the house.

Jay couldn't concentrate on anything the whole day. All he could think of was the car. As he was about to leave for home after classes got over, Alekh called him aside. 'Jay, I know you are upset because your dad won't allow you to take the car out for a drive.' Jay looked down, dejected. 'But there are other ways of doing it, aren't there?' There was a twinkle in Alekh's eyes.

Jay looked up at him, puzzled. 'What do you mean?' he asked.

'Simple,' replied Alekh. 'Let's take your car out for a spin tonight.'

'Tonight?'

'Yup. Slip out of the house with the car keys once everyone's fast asleep. Let's go for a midnight thrill ride.'

'Oh! Okay!' Jay said excitedly.

He returned home feeling happy for the first time in the whole day.

'Jay, come here, Sharma ji, your grand uncle, has come to see you. Go do a namaskar and take his blessings,' his mom called out. Jay was not sure he knew who the gentleman was, but he went in all the same. He was surprised to see an old man sitting on the sofa. He went and touched his feet. The old man patted his back and made him sit next to him.

'Uncle, be comfortable. I will bring tea,' said Jay's mom, and went inside.

'Son, I have a birthday gift for you,' he beamed at Jay.

Jay was least interested. 'You shouldn't have...' Jay began politely, but the old man smiled and took out an old withered pouch from his pocket. He placed it in Jay's hand. Jay opened it and found a wristwatch. It looked very different, something he had never seen before. The dial was a big rectangle with numbers from one to twelve marked along the margins. In between there were three boxes, each of which displayed the date, month and year. Another small box beneath had letters written inside.

'Enter your name in that box. Here... let me show you how to do that.' The old man showed him how and Jay followed his instructions. 'This is a very special watch.

You will soon find out why it is special. Use it to the best and you will make a good life for yourself.' Jay thanked the old man and went up to his room.

As Jay lay in bed, waiting for the clock to strike midnight, he noticed the weird watch on his wrist. He was still intrigued by the old man. Jay started playing with the dials and buttons on the display absent-mindedly. How he wished he was ten years older with no one dictating what he could do and what he couldn't. Then he had an idea. Maybe if he changed the date on the watch he would feel like an adult who was in control of his own life! He set the date to 2 June 2026.

◆

Jay did not know when he had dozed off. When he opened his eyes, the room was bright. It was morning. *Oh no! Alekh must have waited for him!* He sat up and looked around. The room seemed different. The bed was neatly made, but there were no pillows, not even a blanket. The study table, which was usually piled with books and his project material was clear. There was a fine layer of dust on it. The walls, which had been recently painted looked faded and the paint had peeled off in many places. Jay could not believe it. How could the room change overnight? He got out of bed and opened his cupboard. It was completely empty. No clothes. No books. What the hell was going on? And that was when it clicked. The watch. He had set the date on it to 2 June 2026. His birthday! So had he also grown ten years older? Panicking, he rushed to look at himself in the mirror. But the reflection showed him just like he was. The sixteen year old. So what was this? Had he time-travelled?

Jay came out into the living room. The whole house seemed to have aged. Nothing was clean and tidy, the way his mom kept it. It looked like it hadn't been cleaned in ages. The walls were stripped of all of the family photographs. He couldn't understand what had happened. Then he caught sight of his dad sleeping on the sofa. He looked more than ten years older. He was thinner and seemed frail. There were dark circles underneath his eyes and wrinkles all over his hands. Jay swallowed hard. Where was Mom? Had something happened to her? Just then his dad stirred. Jay quickly hid behind a curtain. He didn't want to alarm his father. Why hadn't he himself aged, Jay wondered? Or had he finally fulfilled his dream of getting a job in the US? Probably his twenty-six-year-old self was living in the US. A moment later, his dad got up. He walked with a limp, Jay noticed, and felt bad to see him in such a state. He remained hidden while his dad got ready, and went out of the house. There was no car outside. His dad hailed an auto and got in. Jay immediately got into another auto and began to follow him. Had my dad sold his car to fund my US dream?

To Jay's utter astonishment, his dad stopped in front of a mental asylum. What did his dad have to do here, he wondered. Staying in the shadows, he followed his dad to the reception desk. The lady gave him a sympathetic nod before going back to her paperwork. What was going on? Was his mom here? Slowly a tight knot began to form in Jay's stomach. He saw his dad entering a room. He peered through a crack in the door. The sight made him almost scream in horror.

His mom was sitting on a bed, staring into space. Her hair was dishevelled, her face looked ravaged, like she had aged twenty years. She turned to Jay's dad and with an insane glint in her eyes, said, 'Arun, did you bring Jay back? Today is his birthday. I want to make his favourite vanilla pudding.'

His dad took a deep breath, held her hand, and said, 'Asha, Jay is dead. He died on the night of his sixteenth birthday. He died while driving our car on the highway. We were sleeping peacefully at home. Accept it. The sooner you accept it, the better it will be for both of us. It's been ten years!' His dad began to sob, his chest heaving, shoulders shaking.

'No!' his mother screamed, 'No, Jay! You are not dead! You cannot be dead! Your mom is waiting for you,' she wailed. Jay stood there, stunned. What had he done! What had he done to his parents' lives for just a moment of thrill! Did they deserve this?

The loud ring of his mobile phone woke Jay from his deep sleep. He was sweating. 'Hello?' he managed, still getting oriented to his surroundings.

'It's 12.30. Come down fast, we are waiting for you,' Alekh sounded excited.

'No, Alekh, I am not coming.'

'What? Are you mad or what? Rahul and Atin are also here. Come on, hurry up.' There was impatience in Alekh's tone.

'I am not coming, and I don't think you should go either. Driving can wait. We can do that after we get a proper license. It's only two years away, anyway.'

'Oh, looks like you've just received another sermon from your parents. You are going to repent for not coming,' Alekh said tauntingly and disconnected.

Jay knew what he would repent more.

ONE BAD TURN

Meera Rajagopalan

Winner of the first prize of the #HASJ contest

SLASHING YOUR WRISTS ISN'T AS EASY AS IT LOOKS in the movies. Trust me, I know. By the time you get the nerve to actually pick up the rusted cutter from your son's now-disused toolbox, your heart is beating so wildly that you wonder whether it would simply burst and splatter red all over the house, like the pooshanikkai[1] that's burst to ward off evil.

The blade then feels cool, cool like the spirit they smear on your skin before they operate.

When you finally muster the courage to place the sharp edge on your skin, your eyes automatically close, like they do when you kiss someone. And before you know it, you force your pathetic life to flash before your eyes, looking for that elusive something that will make living

---

[1]Ash gourd. To ward off the evil eye, kumkum is filled in the ash gourd and it is smashed typically in front of business premises and vehicles.

worthwhile. Halfway through, the door bursts open and your daughter-in-law appears, acts shocked, and ululates a bit prematurely, inviting the whole kuppam to watch your humiliation complete.

'What bad name he wants to bring to me,' she cries. 'So everyone will say I didn't take care of him. I've been washing his shit-stained sheets, will anyone talk about that?'

When your son ambles in, his beer-breath making its way to you, through the layers of shame you are still swathed in, you can hear their conversations amplified like the rain on tin roofs. 'He should have died on the road itself,' he finally declares as your daughter-in-law cries. You agree but remain silent.

Out of the corner of your eye, you spot your grandson, barely two, standing in one corner, his lips curved into an arc of disgust.

◆

It was exactly three months ago, on Vijayadasami. My tea shop, lovingly named after my wife, whose love seemed to have disappeared just before she did, was all decked up. My son had left for his mechanic shop, and Radha Tea Stall, for once, smelled of sandal and agarbatti, and not the nauseating mix of nicotine and discarded tea leaves that I thought I was immune to.

The day was dedicated to my trade; my source of livelihood. It was not rocket science, running a teashop.

But it was my source of livelihood and this day was dedicated to its success. It had been this way from the start... men came and men went, day in and day out... but my task remained the same... pretty much like the Earth going round and round in its orbit, and rotating on its axis.

That evening, it had started to drizzle. I wanted to go home as soon as I could—my daughter-in-law would have been tired, running around the whole day, (and would need help with her kids—Mani, two, and Velammal, six.

Just as I was leaving, the clouds had started to spit out the rain faster, as if angry that earthlings had not taken the drizzle seriously, much like Mani's tantrums. As I climbed on to my trusted TVS Champ, whose idiosyncrasies and moods only I could decipher, I felt at home. I couldn't wait to see Mani; he had been running a fever for the past two days. The rain was coming down in torrents when I passed the Koyambedu bus stand. I was drenched. I could barely see ahead. I thought of stopping for shelter when I felt my phone vibrate in my pocket. It was my daughter-in-law.

'Mama,' she screamed, 'Mani's fever has not come down at all. Please come home soon.'

Try as I might, I am unable to recall anything about that night except the thought that the one-way street would add precious minutes to my commute. When I woke up, they said it was two days later, my son and daughter-in-law were by my side. They were relieved to see me open my eyes. I drifted right back to sleep. This went on for a couple of days. Every time I opened my eyes for a brief while, I saw them in varying moods—ranging from relief to anxiety to irritation and then plain cold anger.

The doctors came and went, groups of students surrounded senior doctors, who treated my body as a cadaver and the stinking general ward for men (accidents), as a classroom. Nearly all the bones in the lower half of my body were broken when the lorry ran over my legs. An operation was scheduled for when my body would be able take it. It would cost money, though. Not much, it was the free hospital, after all.

An official-looking man came to my bedside and took my statement. A statement I couldn't give properly because my son was constantly interrupting me. I told the man all that I remembered. Yes, I said, my grandson was very ill... As soon as the man left, my son pounced on me, his face morphing into a grotesque mask.

'How dare you tell him that you were going on the wrong side?' he thundered. 'I told you to let me do the talking a hundred times, but you insisted on opening your mouth!'

I cowered.

'Now we will not get anything.' He continued his rant, 'The lorry guy will go scot-free and we are left with all of this,' he shook a sheaf of papers at my face.

My eyes were becoming heavy and as he came close, I smelled the alcohol. He pried my eyes open. 'Don't you dare sleep!' he shouted, spraying spittle on me. 'You cannot just go to sleep like nothing happened.'

There were a few visitors—the fruit stall woman, the man who ran the shoe shop round the corner, and most surprisingly, the jogger lady with the tick mark on her T-shirt.

She asked after me, and tears welled up in her eyes. I took the money she held out, but before I could put it in my pocket, my son grabbed it from me.

A month and two surgeries later, the doctors gave their verdict: It was unlikely that I would walk again. Perhaps I could, with physiotherapy and some training, but all of that would cost money. They needed the hospital bed for other patients. Others who had better chances of complete recovery, perhaps.

◆

Now, I lay discarded like a banana peel, relegated to a corner of the house.

It has been a week since the botched attempt. My daughter-in-law has managed to get a 'sentry' to ensure I don't get up to do 'silly stuff' again—a lady friend of hers. The rubber sheet feels cool under me. I feel a shot of heat as my piss joins my shit in taunting me from below. I wait an hour, two hours. The sentry will not even touch me.

It is noon when my son walks in. He enters and crinkles up his nose. He asks the lady to leave as he pulls me up and carries me to the makeshift toilet, where he cleans me up and puts powder all over me, like I am a rotting dustbin. He cleans the bed and replaces the sheets. He helps me lie down. He kisses my cheeks. I'm touched. Before he goes, he presses something cold against my palm and closes my fingers over it.

'I'll be back in two hours,' he says.

I open my trembling palm only after he leaves, and find a shimmering new blade, gleaming in the light of the sun that enters through the holes in the tin walls of the house.

THE LIGHT OF HIS EYES

Ratnadip Acharya

As I kick-started my motorbike I looked back over my shoulder, at him, sitting there in that tiny room, with the corrugated cardboard roof. Our eyes met for a brief instant and I could see his eyes glinting with confidence and determination.

My coming to the post office that morning was indeed providential, I thought. Net-banking and excellent courier services had made the existence of a post office somewhat unimportant for me. However, that day I had to send an important document by registered post, and that's why I had gone there. As I was about to leave the post office, a man with an embarrassed smile approached me. He was looking for someone to fill up a money-order form for him. I offered to do it and when I finished filling up the form, to my surprise, he offered me a ten-rupee note. When I refused to accept it he asked me, 'But isn't that the usual charge for filling a form?'

'I don't know,' I replied. But I was curious. 'Who do

you pay ten rupees for filling a money-order form?' I asked him.

He pointed at a man sitting right outside the post office. 'To the man who sits in that small makeshift room. He has a fixed charge for everything, from making a parcel, stitching and sealing it to filling up different kinds of forms. But he is too busy now, so I have come to the post office directly, hoping that someone would help me,' he smiled.

I walked up to my bike and looked around as I put on my helmet. I noticed a tiny shack stuck to the wall of the post office. Two thin plyboard sheets made up the other two walls. The door, also another plywood sheet, was open. I stood on the pavement and looked inside. In this tiny, dingy room, sitting on a straight-back chair behind a rough wooden table was a man whose age was difficult to guess. He had strong shoulders, a broad forehead, a sharp nose and a firm chin. There was a look of determination on his face. He was wearing a T-shirt and a pair of shorts. Both his legs were amputated below the knees. On the wall behind him were photographs, of the man doing all the exercises that someone without legs could do. I stood there watching him busily stitching up a parcel with great dexterity, then writing the name and address on it in a neat handwriting. My curiosity to know more about the man was aroused. When the man with the parcel had gone, I walked into the 'office' room. The man on the chair looked at me.

'How can I help you, Sir?' he asked, looking straight at me.

'Oh, I don't need any help. I was just curious because someone I met at the post office told me that you do this kind of work for a fee. But then I saw the photos and was wondering how to ask you...' I did not complete my sentence because I was embarrassed to mention his legs.

'What? That my legs are amputated?' he said with a smile. After a pause, he added, 'And you must also be wondering why I stuck these photographs on the wall like a show off.' I nodded. 'It is not about blowing my own trumpet, Sir. There is a specific reason for sticking these photographs. If you want to hear the entire story, you have to be with me for another ten to fifteen minutes.' Without a second thought, I settled on the only rickety chair in the room.

'Hope no one comes and interrupts me,' he smiled.

I smiled back. I looked around and noticed a pair of crutches, leaning against the wall beside him. Seeing me looking at the crutches, he gave me a lopsided smile.

'They have been my best friends for the last five years.' Then he began his story. 'I came to Mumbai a good ten years back and after spending a few months wandering around aimlessly, I found the means to a steady income. With the little money I had I bought a hand cart and a manual fruit-juicer. And thus I started selling musambi and pineapple juice in front of this post office. Soon I was friends with the rediwallas nearby. Whether it was a bicycle-repairer, or a barber or a south Indian anna, selling idli and medu vada by the street—we were all friends. I was happy with my life till one day misfortune struck. This road has always had heavy traffic. Truck drivers and motorcyclists are the ones who are most reckless.

'On that fateful day, I was crossing the road cautiously, with a sack full of musambi, when a motorbike came out of nowhere and hit me from behind. I fell right in the middle of the road. I was not too badly hurt and was about to get up when I saw a truck coming at me at lightning speed. Seeing me lying on the road, the driver must have applied the brakes but it was too late. The front tyre had run over my thighs by that time. An excruciating pain blinded me and suddenly everything was blank.' He let out a sigh.

'When I opened my eyes again, there were some blurred images in front of me. Soon they started taking clear shapes. I noticed a film of gloom on the faces of all my friends. They did not tell me, but soon I found out the reason for it. Both my legs had been amputated from the knees.

'For the next few months, days and nights were equally dark for me. Time and again I thought of ending my life. I would spend my days lying on a shaky bed in a squalid room, gazing vacantly at the walls. One day, I observed something very unusual. On one of the walls of my room I saw a moth sitting on the wall and a lizard watching it meditatively. At a propitious moment, it attacked the moth. But the moth was not an easy prey. It didn't give up easily and continued fluttering its wings furiously until the lizard gave up on it. Once the moth won the fight, it shook its wings triumphantly. It struck me that if a moth could fight and set itself free from the jaws of death then I must try to make the most of my life. During the next few days, my belief in my fighting spirit strengthened as I saw the same moth. After a few days, I saw a moth on the wall, but this time the lizard glided about without making any further attempt at attacking it. This insect was a huge inspiration to me.

'Slowly, I started practising to walk with the help of crutches. A couple of months later, I was sitting outside Anna's idli and medu vada stall when a man came asking for assistance to fill up a money-order form. I had studied till eighth standard and could barely write English then. That morning once I filled up that form, an idea started germinating in my mind. And as you can see now, five years have passed since that morning and here I am now. A month of confinement had made me flabby and I was feeling very bad about my body. Then once again inspiration struck me and I started doing exercises that a legless man could do. The result is in front of you,' he breathed deeply and went on. 'One thing I deeply felt, no matter whatever we want to do in life, if our effort is total, desire is earnest, help does come from unknown sources. And once we are grateful to life for giving us another opportunity to live a fulfilling life, we feel like contributing to life at large in whatever limited means we have.'

'I used to sit in my little room and watch so many youngsters riding their vehicles so recklessly as if they care a damn about their own and other peoples' lives. I wanted to do something to make them understand the dangers of reckless driving. I clicked these snaps of myself and pasted them on the plywood. Many people who come to me get curious after seeing these photographs. Whenever an opportunity presents itself, I tell people how someone's reckless driving cost me both my legs. I urge everyone to value others' lives while riding for we are all interconnected on earth. A loss of a life will haunt all of us in some way. If my words can avert a single accident that is a great achievement for me, isn't it, Sir?'

'I have never been so impressed and inspired by anyone in my life,' I told him as I got up.

With a smile he said, 'I sincerely request you to tell my story to everyone you know in whatever way you can. No one else should lose his legs or his life to an accident. Let my tragedy be the last one,' he told me determinedly.

THE GOOD SAMARITANS

Roshan Radhakrishnan

GRIMACING AS THE GLASS OF HOT TEA STUNG MY fingers, I walked towards the last unoccupied bench outside the tea shop. I wanted a few moments to myself, to drink my tea in peace.

As I sat down, I saw a frail old man walking up to random strangers, handing them slips of paper. Curious, I kept watching him. Most of the people either ignored him or took the paper silently and put it in their pockets. A few smiled, nodded and read what was written on it.

After a few moments I went back to my tea, dismissing the man as a donation seeker or a lottery-ticket seller.

Just then, I saw a red sedan stop near my bench. The well-dressed man who alighted from the car was probably a regular customer at this tea stall. As he came up to where I was sitting, the boy from the tea shop came running up to him with two glasses of tea and a loosely wrapped oily paper parcel that did little to hide the contents within.

I looked away as he searched for a seat, knowing well that my bench was the only available option.

'May we sit here?' the man asked me politely. I nodded in reply, looking up to see the cause for the plural. The donation-seeker was standing beside him. He is really quick, I thought to myself. But then, to my surprise, both of them sat down beside me. As I listened to their conversation, it became obvious that the two knew one another. Sharing from the assortment of bhajjis between them, one spoke of people he had approached that day on the streets while the other talked of a client he had met from a foreign company. The oddity of that moment—two people from entirely different worlds, generations, social backgrounds and lifestyles chatting away like good friends was unusual to say the least. Their conversation would come back to haunt me as I drove home later that night.

'So how many papers did you give today, Baba?' the young man asked.

'Ten. Nobody stops to listen anymore.'

'Working in a multinational company, I have the same problem. Education does not imply common sense.'

Intrigued, I craned my neck to peek at the papers placed on the bench beside the old man. When I looked up, the younger man was smiling at me.

'I am sorry. I should not have eavesdropped.' I felt guilty.

'It is okay. Here, take one.' I took the paper he offered me. The paper itself was cut to the size of a hundred-rupee note. Before I could begin reading, the young man started to speak. 'We met two months ago at the casualty department of Baby Memorial Hospital. He was a labourer at a construction site nearby, raising his grandchildren after their mother passed away. They used to study in the primary school close to the beach. This man knew the vagaries of the traffic on the busy road and did his best to make them understand road-safety rules since he could not go to pick up and drop them.' The man took a slow, measured sip from his glass, as though willing it to steel his nerves before continuing. 'The lady driving the car, too, knew the traffic rules well. She just did not have time to react as the bus coming from the opposite direction overtook a bike and came right at her. The impact pitched the car off the road onto the sidewalk where the two children were walking home after school, and crushed them against the wall.'

I turned to the old man. The pain in his eyes confirmed my fears.

'Hundreds passed by but no one came to help. They told reporters they did not want to get involved because they either had places to go to or just did not want to get stuck in the hospital and for police questioning later. And so, because it was an inconvenience for everyone, two innocent children and one young wife died, crying out for their loved ones till their last breath.'

My own eyes watered as I saw a tear roll down the old man's cheek. I looked at the sheet of paper in my hand. On it was an explanation of the new laws to help good Samaritans who come to the aid of strangers during an accident. 'The laws have been amended in 2016, to help Samaritans keep their identity private, to allow them to leave after providing information, assuring them there would be no harassment from the police later on,' the man said. Almost ruefully, he continued, 'Millions go online everyday to check out an actor's love life and cricket-score updates. But nobody thought it was worthwhile to read an amendment that could save the lives of their loved ones.' He paused, for a moment. 'Every four minutes an Indian dies because of a road accident. And every study done says that 50 per cent of those deaths could have been prevented if the victim had received help during the *golden hour*, the critical first hour after the accident.'

I turned the paper over. On the back was a form titled 'My Health Information.' I read it out aloud.

Name:

Age:

Address:

In case of an emergency

Contact (Name/number/relation):

1)

2)

Blood group:

My Ailments:

Current medication (Dosage):

I am allergic to:
THANK YOU FOR HELPING ME.

'What is this?' I asked.

'Initially, we only printed out the Good Samaritan note. Do you know what happened? People threw the notes away. I needed to make people hold onto the paper but I was not succeeding. This meant that someone somewhere was still dying.'

We stood up and as we walked, the corporate professional within him started talking. 'On analysing, I realised why I had failed. We never think an accident can happen to us. That's when I decided to turn the tables. I made everyone a potential victim. When you fill in that form you realise how much you hope somebody will read it and help you. You understand the gravity of a road accident... the level of helplessness. This simple piece of paper can save lives. Your family can be contacted, and the emergency team has your medical history at hand. This is invaluable. It saves time.'

Despite my protests, the young man paid for all of us. I watched as he hugged the old man, whispering something softly in his ears before getting into his car. He nodded to me. 'Take a few more sheets. Fill a form for your parents and keep it in their wallets. It is just a simple note which may never be used. But should the day come, it could be the one note in that wallet that saves them.' His right hand reached out and he waved slowly to me. Even as I reciprocated his gesture, a thought arose within the crevices of my mind and I felt my breath catch as I watched the car drive off, heading towards town. Having placed quite a few papers in my palm, the old man, too, turned and slowly walked away, seeking out new faces in the crowd.

As I rode back home that night, for perhaps the first time in ages, I dutifully wore my helmet. My eyes remained on the road and I waited patiently behind smoke-snorting trucks instead of zigzagging my way past them. My mind, too, was on the road, in a way. I thought of how unforgiving these roads were. They did not see in you a father or a son, a mother or a grandfather. They did not discriminate based on your religion or bank balance. But human beings do. We are supposed to be capable of seeing in every victim our parents, spouse and children. And yet, we do not. We hurry by as a life is extinguished, unwilling to make even a minimal effort for fear we will be inconvenienced. I thought of the old man who had lost his grandchildren. I thought of my own father, his arthritis and eyesight getting worse with every passing year, stepping out of the house in the evening to buy biscuits from a nearby store because he knows I love them. I knew at that moment that I would fill those forms and place them not just in my parents' wallets but also in my own.

I slowed down in front of my colony as my thoughts turned to the man in the red car. I remembered how he talked of his first meeting with the old man at the casualty department of the hospital. I remembered his voice cracking as he described the accident, reliving a memory he was not a witness to. I remembered his words, '...two innocent children and *one young wife* died crying for their loved ones...' I was struck by the realisation of what had linked the two as he waved goodbye—the pale band of skin at the bottom of his fourth finger which had yet to forget the wedding ring it once adorned. I prayed I was wrong but I knew within my soul, the truth of the connection between the two mourners. And as I lay down to sleep that night, I remembered how similar their eyes were; the eyes of two sorrowful strangers whose journeys had intersected so cruelly along the unforgiving road of life.

THE TRUE HERO

Roshni Chhabra

Winner of the third prize of the #HASJ contest

Dharam Singh was waiting anxiously for the phone call.

Tring-tring! 'Hello?'

'Congratulations, your wife has given birth to a baby boy,' announced the doctor. Dharam Singh wasn't able to say anything in reply. He could only feel his eyes water with happiness.

He had lost his first son in a road accident a couple of years ago. The birth of this child would cheer up their lives now, he thought. He took out the picture of his beautiful wife and his first son from his pocket and held it close to his heart. With a prayer and a feeling of gratitude, Dharam Singh hoped that now, for his wife, the pain of having lost her first child would ease somewhat. He returned to the camp and announced to his fellow soldiers that he was a father again. Cheers and congratulatory wishes poured in.

Dharam Singh had not been able to go home to be

with his pregnant wife because he was engaged in a confidential project for the Indian Army. He was a very brave soldier. He had lost his first son, could not attend to his pregnant wife, and now he was not there to see his second son when he arrived in this world. But he was a man who never lost his calm.

When he went home after a month, he was amazed to see that his baby boy looked very much like his first son, Veer. He was almost a doppelganger of Veer. Dharam Singh picked him up from the cradle gently and kissed his forehead. 'Veer. Yes, your name, too, will be Veer,' he whispered. His wife, Poonam, was peeping through the kitchen window. Seeing her husband cuddling the baby, she smiled. What's bred in the bone will come out in the flesh, she thought to herself.

Soon, Dharam Singh had to leave home to get back to where he had been posted. By the time Dharam Singh returned to be with the family, Veer had grown up into a smart young lad. He was just like his father, disciplined and strong. Whenever Dharam Singh was home, he would take Veer on early morning jogs and make him do strenuous exercises. Veer loved sports and did his workout regularly and untiringly. Dharam Singh treasured watching his son breaking a sweat, and often bragged to his friends, 'You see, Veer will definitely be an army officer when he grows up and will protect his motherland, his country.'

As Veer grew older, he often asked his mother about

his brother and why God hadn't saved him. But when he saw his mother getting upset by his questions, he would stop pestering her. He would always say that he wanted to do something in his brother's memory.

As days passed, Veer transformed into a handsome young man with a fine personality. One day, his father said: 'C'mon, son, lace up your boots! The time has come for you to prepare for the SSB exam to get entry into the Indian Army. I know you have been waiting for this.'

But Veer looked at his father with a clear and confident gaze. 'I am sorry, Dad, I don't want to join the Army.'

Dharam Singh was stunned. He couldn't believe what he had just heard. 'Then what do you want to do?' he growled.

'I want to be a traffic policeman.'

'A what? Are you serious? I always thought you would join the Army. Being my son, how can you be so foolish? Have you lost your mind?'

Dharam's wife took her son's side. She understood the motive behind Veer's decision and convinced Dharam to let the boy do what he wanted. But it was not easy for him to accept his son wanting to become a traffic policeman, thinking that his son deserved to get into a much 'better' profession. Now what would he say to his friends? Everyone would laugh at him. Veer, however, was firm about his decision.

He joined the police force and underwent rigorous

training. Soon, he was posted in the Delhi region of National Highway No. 48. Usually, when a son gets employed, the family celebrates. But the atmosphere in Veer's home was nowhere near happy.

Veer did not let all this affect him. He remained calm just like his father used to be during difficult times. He was all set to unbutton the army uniform which his father had made him wear in his imagination and put on the traffic policeman's uniform with pride. And like all loving mothers, when Veer was about to leave for duty on the first day, Poonam came running from the kitchen with a bowl of sweet curd. 'How can you forget to eat sweet curd on your first day.... Here, open your mouth.' She fed him from the bowl and blessed him.

Veer loved his work. He never complained about the busy traffic, the scorching heat or the chilly winds. He would put his heart and soul into preventing and easing chaotic traffic situations. Delhi's infamous pollution, snarling tempers and general unruliness never succeeded in deterring him. For Veer, working as a traffic policeman was his way of paying a tribute to his late brother. Of course, deep inside his heart, he knew that his father was disappointed with him and felt bad about that.

Soon it was August and security was tightened for Independence Day celebrations. Not just in the city but on the highways as well. Newspapers were full of the news of Aarthi Das from India who had been selected as one of the astronauts for the next Mars Mission from

NASA. It was a matter of great pride for the whole country. She was to be felicitated by the president during the Independence Day celebrations at Red Fort. On the evening of 14 August, she was travelling by car to Delhi on National Highway 48. Veer was on duty at that time. He was given special orders by higher authorities to ensure the security of the area. At the quadrilateral, as expected, people had gathered to see Aarthi Das. Policemen had been on duty since the wee hours of the morning to ensure the crowd was restricted to the barricaded area. As Aarthi Das's car was about to take a left turn, Veer noticed a bus hurtling down the road from the opposite side. How could this happen, thought Veer to himself. Elaborate security arrangements had been made to stall traffic from all sides. Veer blew his whistle as loudly as he could and started running towards the bus. On his walkie-talkie, the loud voice of a colleague informed him of a bus that had broken a barricade and in the process injured two constables who were manning it. Veer ran towards the bus, confident that he will be able to stop it. After all, the lives of the passengers on the bus as well as Aarthi Das's were at stake. But the bus driver was drunk and had lost control. In an unexpected turn of events, the bus swerved to the right—the spot where Veer was standing, right in front of a lampost.

'Krchhhhhhh!' The horrific sound of sudden brakes shocked everyone into silence as they turned to see what had happened. Blood was flowing from under the wheels of the bus. An ambulance was called and Veer was immediately rushed to the nearest hospital.

As the news of the accident reached Dharam and his wife, they hurried to the hospital. 'Move! Move!' they cried, pushing aside news reporters and bystanders. 'That's our son!' they screamed.

Dharam Singh saw a stretcher being wheeled in and ran alongside it. 'Everything will be alright, son, don't worry,' he said to the unconscious and bloodied body of Veer as the hospital staff rushed it into the operation theatre.

Dharam Singh and his wife waited outside the operation theatre for the doctors. They had already lost their first son Veer, and were not ready to lose their second Veer as well. The soft sounds of murmured prayers filled the silent waiting room. After a long time, the doctor came out, a dejected look on his face. 'I am really sorry, Mr Singh, but we could not save your son. There was a huge amount of blood loss and also a major head injury.'

Dharam's world shattered when the word sorry reached his ears. He couldn't hear the rest of the doctor's statement. But he did not cry. For the first time, he realised that what his son had done was no less than what a soldier at the border does for his country. Even in that state of utter shock and misery, Dharam realised that his son had lost his life only to save the lives of many others. Outside the hospital, reporters surrounded him and his wife. His wife tried to shoo them away, saying they needed time. But Dharam Singh told one of the reporters in a calm and composed voice, 'Every day, around 3000 people die in road accidents. My son prevented one such major accident by sacrificing his own life. In fact, every traffic policeman out there is no less than a hero. They risk their lives everyday to make your lives safer. Today, I salute all members of the traffic police and request all Indians to follow traffic rules, obey instructions given by the traffic policemen and respect their sacrifices for the sake of the safety of the citizens.' After a small pause, he said in a voice choked with emotion, 'I proudly say that I am the father of a traffic policeman.'

WHAT CAN I DO?

Sahar Fatima

Winner of the second prize of the #HASJ contest

'THERE IT IS, SIR, DO YOU SEE IT?' THE NERVOUS secretary pointed at the apparition on his screen. Hari was annoyed; it was almost midnight, and he was still in office.

'A shadow... a trick of the light. It is nothing. Happens all the time on CCTV recordings.'

'Every night, same time? How is it possible, Sir?' the young man persisted.

'Some glitch in the software, maybe. I tell you what, it is too late in the night to be thinking of ghosts, it gives me the heebie-jeebies. I will look at it first thing in the morning.' Hari got up, adjusting his waistband over his considerable girth.

'I just...' The secretary hesitated. His boss was most probably right, and there was no harm in making the dead wait another night.

'Goodnight, you better get home too,' Hari said as he went down to the parking lot. Just as Hari was about to drive out he saw an extraordinary sight—his secretary was leaning out of the office window, waving and yelling at him. 'What?' Hari stopped the car and shouted back, more than a little annoyed now.

Jaaayy Ceee Road was all he could make out. Hari chuckled and waved back. He was quite amused with his assistant's solicitude. JC Road appeared harmless enough to Hari. It was a motorist's delight and Delhi Police's nightmare. Every other night, a gang of over-excited teenagers performed wheelies and unimaginable stunts there on their superbikes which often resulted in broken bones, crippling spinal injuries, even death. It was ironic, Hari thought, that most of these murderous machines were birthday presents from irresponsible parents. 'Screeeeeecchhhh!' Hari brought his car to a skidding halt as he spotted something in front of him. Where had the girl come from? If it were not for his super-cop instincts, he would have run straight into her. She stood in the middle of the road in tattered clothes; a soft wind billowing her hair. Words ran through his mind:

Sixteen. Slum dweller. Shocked. Bleeding. Dead. He shook the last word out of his brain.

She was knocking on the passenger window now. Hari rolled it down. 'Can I come in?' she asked. Hari considered his options. The road was deserted; there was not a soul in sight. He was a cop; he could not possibly just drive away. Besides, he reminded himself, this stretch of road had CCTV cameras. He let her in.

'I was waiting for you. It has been a long time since I crossed over, but I never found you,' said the girl.

'Mmmeee?' Hari gulped, 'What do you want from me?'

'Well, you are from the police, aren't you?'

'No, not really. Just traffic police. How did you get hurt? Can I drive you to the hospital?'

'Doctors cannot help me now. Don't you see?' She pointed to the gash across her stomach; raw red blood oozed out of it.

'It is a fresh wound, not too bad.' Hari judged her professionally. 'The flow can still be checked. Let me take you to the hospital.'

The girl's voice was pitiable. 'They left me here. Many cars came this way, they saw me, but no one stopped. An old lady came to me and told me she had called the ambulance. I begged her to take me to the hospital, *please, please, please,* I said. She hesitated, the man with her said that the car seats would be ruined with blood stains. He said the car costed fifty lakhs. I suppose fifty lakhs is a huge amount?' she spoke wistfully.

Hari took the opportunity to look at her again. Her pupils were glassy marbles set in an icy field, her face had the texture of withered autumn leaves. Hari braced himself to the undisputable fact that he was stuck in the car with a ghost. 'Yes, it is a huge amount for some. But not so much for others.'

'Oh,' the girl said and was quiet for some time.

'Okay, I am the police in some way. What do you

want from me? Do you remember the number plate of the car that hit you? Just tell me the registration number, and I swear on Durga Maiya, I will ensure they serve a life sentence. You will never have to visit me again. I will make it my life's mission to hunt them down on your behalf,' Hari swore quite passionately and even believed it too. At that moment, he felt somewhat like Akshay Kumar or Salman Khan out to avenge a damsel in distress.

'I do not want revenge; the dead do not feel that way. Those feelings are for the living. But I am glad you want to help me. I wonder why people are afraid of the police if they are like you.' She looked at him in an admiring sort of way, which was admittedly quite creepy.

'Well, then what do you want? Hurry up, I don't have all day,' Hari spat out, more out of habit.

'You see, it is a little crowded,' the girl whispered, a little intimidated by his brusque attitude. Hari looked at the road through the windshield and gasped. The earlier empty cement road which shone like a black diamond under the yellow streetlights was now crammed with people. Not a single inch of its surface was visible. A sea of humanity stood in front of him, all facing him, rich folks and poor ones, males and females and lots of children. Their hair was dusty, clothes a little torn, scratched and cut, blood oozing from their wounds. They looked at him with lifeless eyes just like the girl next to him, and they all stood as if they were demanding something from him. Hari was not easily fazed. As a policeman, he was accustomed to blood and gore, but even so, his stomach churned at the horrendous sight and he couldn't utter a single word.

'They all died on this road,' the girl offered by way of explanation. 'Some were crossing the road without looking, others were in their vehicles, driving too fast. Some were in the wrong, most weren't.'

So many dying on this road alone? It is not possible, Hari thought, yet he realised it was indeed quite possible.

'The only thing we have in common is that we all led promising lives which were cut unnaturally short by an avoidable accident. Our loved ones still cannot believe it; they hold on to us, in their memories we linger on. And a new soul, sometimes more, comes to us every day and we fill up. The land of the dead doesn't exactly have highrises you see,' the girl trailed off.

'What can I do? It is not my fault,' Hari told her a little defensively. He hadn't killed those people.

'*What can I do?* They said it too,' the girl murmured.

'Who?'

'Those I met here and talked to about the state of affairs. One man said that he was just a regular commuter and blamed the infrastructure. He told me to meet a politician. Now that was not easy, let me tell you. They have a large fleet of cars accompanying them, but I did meet him. The politician felt the common man needed to follow the rules and regulations strictly. He directed me to an RTO officer and so I went, from pillar to post.

Finally someone said it is the traffic police commissioner who can resolve the issue, so here I am.'

Hari cursed under his breath. There had been many times he had grudged reporting to ministers; he had never in the wildest of his dreams imagined reporting to a ghost too!

Suddenly, Hari came up with an idea. 'Hmm. I don't know what we can do. We have put up billboards. We have run TV advertisements and installed traffic signs. But that doesn't seem to be enough.' He thought for a while. 'What this road needs is a footpath. See, there is no place for pedestrians to walk. Invariably, they come in the way of the vehicles. Now if you will just wait a minute, I will give you the registration number of the PWD chief engineer's car. He will be able to help you.'

MEMORIES

Sanket Chaudhury

When the news reached Arya, it did not shock her. Her grandfather had been near the end of his fight with cancer. She had spent weeks in preparation for this day but she still felt a sort of emptiness, like a part of her had gone missing. Knowing that all she had now were the memories she had created with him. As she walked towards her car in the parking lot at the hospital, she could not help reminisce about the amazing moments associated with this very car. It had been a gift from her grandfather on her nineteenth birthday. Arya's mother was not very pleased; but Grandpa cheerfully reminded her mom that her own mother's disapproval had not prevented her from owning a car at the same age.

Arya turned on the ignition and remembered how she had once received a call from him at midnight. He had only said, 'Come see me, now.' Arya had reached his house as quickly as possible, nervous and anxious, only to find him perfectly well and fully dressed for that late hour. He wanted to drive to a hill station nearby, because Arya's mother was out of town and would not be able to stop them. At that moment, Arya realised what her grandfather was up to. Arya was a literature student and a budding writer, but for the past few months, she had been suffering from writer's block. Her grandfather was aware of what she was going through, and this was his way of cheering her up, and she was grateful.

It was a trademark Arya-Grandpa trip. They used to do this every Saturday. The two of them would set off, driving wherever their fancy took them, stopping whenever they felt like it—for food, or to admire the scenery. They would watch movies together, and discuss their favourite books. They would go to grocery shops and load up carts with junk food, things they weren't allowed to purchase, then leave the loaded carts in the aisles feeling strangely satisfied and yet guilty for having increased the workload of the poor staff.

Arya's grandfather had been the coolest person she had ever known. In spite of the tragedies he'd suffered in his life, he had been most jovial and enjoyed life to the fullest. Arya's grandmother had lost her life in a road accident. It had not been his fault, yet he gave up driving, something he had loved doing. But he loved road trips, only, he was extremely cautious. He would constantly remind Arya to put on her seat belt, turn on the indicator before making turns, check mirrors, adjust the seat, and things like that... Instructions most people knew but often ignored. It had become second nature for Arya to follow them. Grandpa always said those were the little things that save one's life.

Revelling in these reminiscences, Arya noticed that her car needed fuel and headed to a petrol pump. As she was about to drive out, she realised she would never visit it again with her grandfather. It seemed silly, for it was just a petrol pump, but the thought made her emotional. She gathered herself together and looked down. She had forgotten to wear the seatbelt! As she buckled up, she remembered the time when he was teaching her how to drive. She would always turn on the ignition as soon as she got into the car, forgetting to put on the seatbelt, and he would gently chide her and say, 'Arya, once the car gets moving, the thrill of driving makes you forget everything. That's why one must make sure everything is done before you start driving. It does not take a lot of effort to first put on your seatbelt, check the mirrors and adjust your seat before turning on the engine. Why must we be in such a hurry to go through life?'

Arya would smile and reply, 'Master Yoda, the truth you speak. Follow your instructions, I must.' Then they would laugh. These foundational teachings were what had made Arya such a good driver.

Smiling to herself at the thought, Arya looked in the rearview mirror and suddenly noticed a truck catching up on her rapidly. Arya, who was driving in the right lane, decided to move left, to allow the truck passage.

But when she looked again, she saw that it was almost on her tail and right between both lanes, leaving Arya nowhere to go. She tried speeding up but it was of no use, he was approaching too fast. Just as Arya braced for impact, the truck rammed into the back of her car, sending it spinning into the street light right next to the road.

'Arya, my brave, wonderful girl,' said her grandfather as Arya opened her eyes. She saw whiteness all around, and in the middle, her grandpa's face smiling at her.

'Grandpa? What are you doing here? I thought you were... they said....' words failed Arya.

'If you are referring to my death, it certainly did happen,' he replied, smiling ethereally.

'So am I also... you know... dead?' asked Arya uncertainly.

'I do want you to join me in the afterlife but not so soon. What kind of Master Yoda wishes Luke to go with him? Nah... you're alive, and I am so proud of you. You did everything right. You followed all the rules, and see, here you are.'

'I only did what you had dinned into me, Grandpa, so, I should be thanking you.'

'It's easy to teach, Arya, but difficult to follow advice. I should know. If only I had followed it, your grandmother would be alive,' he said, his smile tinged with melancholy.

Arya again felt words failing her. She just lay there looking at her grandfather, wondering if this was some real conversation they had had in the past which her subconscious was replaying for her.

'So you left, huh? What am I supposed to do on Saturdays now?' asked Arya after what seemed like ages.

'Do what a normal twenty-five-year-old would, Arya, and get yourself a date on Saturday,' said Grandpa, his smile turning mischievous.

'Grandpa! Seriously... are we going to discuss my love life right now?' asked Arya indignantly.

'Well, I am supposed to leave soon, I thought I'd bring it up one last time. Can't hurt to try, eh?' he laughed.

'Do you really have to go?' asked Arya.

'Well, I don't have to. But you do, child,' he replied.

As Arya opened her eyes, she saw her mom gasping in delight. 'Oh, Arya! I was so worried. When the call came in, I almost broke down. Losing your grandpa and then being told you had had an accident. I was so worried! You two always ganged up on me but this is ridiculous.'

'Ma! Relax, I am fine. What did the doctor say?' asked Arya.

'He said it had been a close shave. Just a few bruises on your ribs and collarbone. The truck driver was drunk, probably fell asleep. The fireman who pulled you out said you were lucky. The speed with which he hit you... anything could have happened! Thank god you had your seatbelt on.'

'It's not luck, Ma, it's all because of Grandpa. I remember everything he taught me about switching lanes, maintaining speed, allowing others to pass, everything. Wearing a seatbelt is just the first of it.'

'Well, thank god for your grandpa's teaching then,' said her mother, gently caressing Arya's hair and face.

'I have thanked Grandpa already. Can you believe he said I should go out on dates on Saturday when I asked him what I was supposed to do without him?' Arya exclaimed with a touch of disdain in her voice.

'Grandpa said what... ? Arya, are you feeling alright? Do you remember where you were before the accident happened? Should I call the doctor?' Arya's mother asked rapidly, her face full of concern.

'No, Ma, I know where I was. I met Grandpa though, just now.' Arya knew fully well this was doing nothing to reassure her mother.

'Just now? Grandpa...? What are you saying? I am going to call the doctor.' Arya's mother was eyeing her closely, and it was evident that she had started panicking.

'Really, Ma, I am fine. Call the doctor if it makes you feel better. I am just saying I said my goodbyes to Grandpa, and thanked him for saving my life.'

'Arya, are you sure this is all real or did it happen in your head?' Arya's mother knew that she had not suffered from memory loss... the doctor had assured her. But after listening to Arya talk like this, she started wondering all over again.

'Of course it happened in my head. But that's no reason for it to not be real,' smiled Arya, putting her mother's fears to rest. Arya giggled to herself, imagining what her grandfather would say if he heard how she referenced their surreal meeting with a Harry Potter quote.

'Okay, you better get some rest now. Your grandfather and his constant vigilance on the road paid off for you big time today,' quipped her mom, turning off the light and heading out of the hospital room.

'Ma, did you just use a Harry Potter reference to point out road safety?' Arya couldn't believe her ears!

'Maybe I did, maybe I didn't,' replied Arya's mom, smiling for the first time. 'Now sleep tight, Harry.'

HAPPY BIRTHDAY

Taamra Segal

Meera opened her eyes and knew it was a special day. It was her daughter's birthday today, and as she got out of bed and looked out of the window, she knew it was going to be a beautiful day. With a smile on her face, Meera began her day as she usually did, getting dressed and making breakfast. While she ate, her mind was busy going through the list of things she had to do—preparations for the birthday of her only child.

Her daughter's favourite bakery was on the other side of town, so she had to plan her commute accordingly. There was a lot to be done today and she wanted to return home in time.

Ice-cream chocolate truffle cake. That was her daughter's choice of birthday cake every single year. She was just like her mother; once she began to enjoy something, she would stick to it. Whenever they ate at restaurants, both would order their same favourite dish every time.

How time flies, thought Meera, as she brushed her hair in front of the mirror. It felt like only yesterday when she had been handed her little bundle of joy at the hospital. Her daughter had been an easy baby to deliver; she didn't cause much pain to her mother. And Meera mentioned this every year on her daughter's birthday. The baby was a beautiful one and when she grabbed her mother's finger with her tiny ones, it seemed to Meera that she smiled at her. She couldn't believe this miracle was one she had created. Thinking of her baby now, twenty-one years later, she wondered to herself how time had flown.

Meera thought of her daughter's wedding. What would it be like? What would the man she chose to marry be like? And then Meera thought of the grandchildren she would have one day and how she would play with them. I wonder if they will look like me at all? Will they have their grandfather's stubborn streak? Will they be girls or boys? The thought made her smile.

All of a sudden, she thought she heard sirens from down the street and glanced outside her bedroom window.

Nothing.

Shaking her head, Meera set out on her errands. It was afternoon by then. Within a short while, she was in her car, driving to the bakery. It really was a beautiful day. It was as if the sun was extra bright today in honour of her daughter's birthday. She remembered the time she suggested teaching her daughter how to drive and how she had just smiled and said, 'No, Mom, I don't want to drive. I have you to take me around. I couldn't possibly drive as well as you do.'

Meera was approaching the bakery. It was a little old building on a busy high street but it produced some amazing cakes, pastries and every other baked delicacy imaginable. The building was painted bright pink and in fact, that is how they came upon it one sunny day, eight years ago. Meera had been driving and her daughter was looking out of the window when she saw the building.

'Mom, look! A pink bakery!' she had exclaimed. 'Can we go in, please, please, please?'

Unable to say no to such wide-eyed enthusiasm, Meera had agreed and they had stepped inside. The floors had light pink tiles while the walls were painted in a slightly darker pink with white stripes. Truly a pink paradise. Her daughter couldn't stop gaping in sheer delight at everything she saw inside. After ordering two slices of ice-cream cake, they had settled into one of the pretty pink booths. They never stopped going there after that, and every year, the same delicious ice-cream cake made an appearance on her daughter's birthday.

Meera parked her car outside the bakery and once inside, she was told that her cake was almost ready. She walked around the bakery, looking for some snacks that would complement the cake. A birthday feast indeed!

As she strolled past the glass counter lined with several baked goodies, she glanced around and saw that the floor was still pink, the walls were still striped. Something was different though, but she couldn't put her finger on it. Meera thought she heard the faint sound of sirens outside. She glanced towards the glass door at the front entrance but the street outside was empty.

'Ice cream cake for Meera!'

She snapped out of her reverie, collected the cake and paid for the other snacks. It was getting late, and she was in a hurry to get home. She didn't want it to be too dark by the time she got everything ready at home. She drove at a speed higher than normal, almost hitting a stray dog that ran across the road. Braking sharply, she felt confused—her heart was racing and her forehead drenched in sweat. When she looked in the rearview mirror, she saw the dog happily running on to the other side of the road.

Finally, she made it home. Getting all the goodies out of the bags, she began setting the table. So much delicious food! And then the cake. What's a birthday without cake. Finally, everything was perfect, it was 8 o'clock and Meera was ready.

Sitting down at the table, she looked at the plate she had placed in front of her. It was time. She knew what she had to do... knew it from the minute she woke up that morning, from the moment she sat down at the table laden with food. She finally tore her eyes away from her plate and looked across the table to where her daughter sat.

Except that the chair was empty. The entire room was empty, and silent. The silence was deafening, even the ticking of the clock couldn't be heard. The ice-cream cake began to silently melt, a grotesque pool steadily forming in the centre of the table. Meera was unable to swallow. It was as if time had stood completely still. Frozen.

The only sound she could hear was the sound of her heart beating against her chest. It was getting louder, until suddenly, with a deafening burst, it transformed into the sound of the sirens. It was deafening. With the blaring sirens, the whole room was flooded with blinding red light.

Meera was back at that junction, the place where her world had ended three years ago. Meera was screaming as she was being restrained by police officers who wouldn't let her approach the mangled wreckage. She kicked and screamed and cried, but all she could see was the ambulance with its red lights and the shrieking sirens. Sirens everywhere.

Just a few feet from her was the heap of twisted metal, and in it lay her daughter.

Driving home with her best friend after dinner, they were passing by an intersection where a drunk driver had rammed his car into them head-on. Neither of the girls had any chance of surviving the impact.

The man behind the wheel had been celebrating a friend's engagement with a whole bottle of whiskey and had decided to drive home in spite of that. The music blaring out of his car had continued to play even after the crash. Meera was told all this later.

They had not allowed Meera to see her daughter, so bad was the impact. Her last memory was of her beautiful child from earlier that evening, smiling and waving as she said 'Bye' just before Meera shut the door. Later, she was handed a gold bracelet that was retrieved from her daughter's wrist. It was a present that Meera had given her on her eighteenth birthday. Ever since the accident, Meera had worn it every single day and was wearing it now.

Meera felt she was drowning in sadness, she was choking, but no tears would come.

She couldn't say her daughter's name anymore. Finally, she turned over the bracelet and looked at the engraving:

Happy Birthday, Priya. Love, Mom.

HIGHWAY 666

Thommen Jose

Satan was worried. The deadline for completing the prestigious Hell Highway 666 was fast approaching and the work was going nowhere. The highway, coming up on the last remaining patch of greenery, saw many workers hospitalised because of the clean air. This had led to a grievous labour shortage. The problem had been reported many times but had not been rectified so far.

So this time instead of sending his trusted chief whip, Satan went personally to meet Demon who had charge of the Death Department. Everyone in the department including Demon shuddered with fear on seeing Satan in their midst. The soft clattering of keypads froze and the bit-apple logos on their Macs shone with a menacing brightness. Satan walked into Demon's cabin, munching on something, the blood dripping from his fangs. He asked Demon for the latest reports and specifically, the day's quota from India. Satan was partial towards India numbers as the chances of getting skilled workers was high, thanks to all the construction going on there. Demon pressed some keys which sounded like thunder in the cathedral silence.

'Sir, statistically we are getting a minimum of seventeen people every day,' Demon stammered out. 'But, er... there are only two who will be of any use for the road work,' he added.

Satan flung the rest of his snack into the dustbin, leaving a trail of blood across the hall. A cat hiding in the air conditioning duct above meowed, its glittering green eyes following the red droplets. Satan watched as Demon pressed more keys and two faces popped up. One was of a young man in an expensive leather jacket and the other a wiry, middle-aged one in a moth-eaten vest.

Satan was mildly curious about the obvious difference in the social status of the two men. But he was more interested in getting results.

'Demon,' he said, 'I rarely ask how you conduct your business but consider it the need of the hour or maybe just curiosity. I want to know how you zero in on your candidates.'

'Sir, the man in the vest is a lorry driver with almost two decades of experience,' Demon explained, still extremely nervous, but warming up to the rare attention bestowed on him.

'With a little training he can be used as machine operator for the paving work that should begin next week. The department told me they had a shortage of workforce there.'

'And the leather jacket?'

Demon placed the cursor on the young lad's face, pressed the enter key and started humming a song while reading the details that faded over the photograph but checked himself in time.

'He is the only son of a billionaire builder,' Demon announced before turning his gaze back to the screen. 'Tonight is his twenty-first birthday and the boy is getting an Aventador.' Demon whistled softly and Satan looked at him quizzically.

'It's the newest Lamborghini, Sir. Apparently, only ten of them have been earmarked for India. It hits 100 kmph in under three seconds.' The detailed explanation was probably a consequence of his work; Demon was an accidental petrol head, interested in cars and bikes—the faster they were, the more he loved them.

Before Demon could venture more details on the supercar, Satan thundered. 'Do I look like I care a rat's ass whether he drives an Aventador or a Hero Honda Splendor?'

Demon buckled with fear and fell on the floor in a heap and had to be helped up by his colleagues.

'Just tell me,' Satan hissed at Demon, as he was being hoisted up, 'how is this punk suited for my *work?*'

'Sir,' Demon spluttered, 'he is just back from an electrical engineering course in the UK. I... I thought he might be handy for supervising the laying of cat's eyes on the highway.'

'I want no hiccups here,' Satan said, noticeably calmer. 'Tell me how you are going to do it.'

'Sir, the truck driver is getting drunk now at a dhaba outside Delhi and once the curfew lifts, he will be driving through the city and onwards to Jaipur. The boy is partying at a Saket pub like there is, er, no tomorrow. The truck will have a breakdown on the airport flyover and the boy will ram it from behind at high speed and die on the spot. People will gather and upon finding the lorry driver drunk, they will lynch him.'

'You have a penchant for lynching,' smiled Satan, trying to ease the tense atmosphere.

'Sir, it's fun watching,' piped up the IT head, a woman who had infested millions of computers with more viral strains than found in the rivers next to pharma companies. She had arrived just a month ago and had already burned down the firewalls of all the computers in hell. She held a lot of promise.

Satan glanced at her briefly and left. He had many other things to attend to—a potential construction contractor was on the way. He had just received over WhatsApp a screen shot of the ECG machine at the hospital where the ex PWD chief was lodged. Thanks to a lifetime of corruption and allied worrying, he was well on his way.

A new night blanketed Hell with darkness and very

soon, the contractor reached and immediately reported for duty at Satan's door.

'Sir, let's chuck the compaction work—we can always blame the heavy, untimely rains. I'm thinking of stopping the concrete filling of the joints and doing away with the priming coat on the steel work. We save quite a bundle here and will divide it between us.'

What a way to begin the night, thought Satan and waved the contractor away with a silent nod and a smile.

But the other two workers hadn't come in yet. After waiting an hour Satan stormed into the Death Department once more and demanded an explanation for the delay.

The worst fears of the entire department had come true in this case. Holding out a report with trembling hands, Demon managed to stutter, 'Sir, karmic intervention.'

Satan was stumped.

'Impossible!' he roared. The cat watching through the vent in the ceiling slunk away into the darker recesses of the hidden passage.

Largely due to his inability to speak and partly protocol, Demon took a printout of the report. It was a substantial procedural failure. According to the report, the rich boy's mother had offered a puja at their home shrine while the boy was having fun with his friends. She was still praying for him when she finally retired for the night after a futile wait for him to return home. A starred section in the report pointed out that while the boy was staggering towards his car, Demon even devised a plan to make the friends taunt the boy into a race. (Starred sections play a vital role in annual appraisals, you see.) The boy was caught between the giggling girls tugging at his sleeve and some voice in his head. Finally, he called a radio cab and went home.

Impatient with the details of the report, Satan now opted for the playback from the menu.

The trucker's story came alive on the screen. The drunken driver is being supported to the cabin by his chotu, the helper, when he gets a call from his daughter. The screen splits into two halves—one with the man outside his truck on the outskirts of Delhi and the other with the daughter in a one-room shanty near Patna.

Trucker: 'Yes, my princess, Papa will bring you a puppet doll from Jaipur. Does your mother want anything?'

Daughter: 'She will want her usual chudi and bindi. Papa, I will wait for you and pray you reach me fast and safe.'

Demon looked at Satan, helplessness writ all over his face.

'Sir, the kid's "I'll pray you reach safe" is what messed with our codes,' he managed to mumble.

Satan looked around and saw the IT head lost in thought. He called her over.

'You have to rewrite the programme codes,' he ordered.

She kept staring at him blankly and didn't say anything. He then remembered her competencies lay in spreading binary filth and not writing useful codes. He had to do the job himself. Satan sat there, stroking his pointy chin till his LED eyes glinted. Soon, his fangs were bared in a grin. Everybody around knew it would be a masterstroke.

'Rework the algorithms,' Satan said in a hoarse whisper, 'in such a way that it shows those who drink while they drive are those who don't care for anybody but themselves. And make those idiots *think* there's nobody who cares for them even if there really are. In short, make drinking and driving not just stupid but purely selfish.'

Everyone gathered around Satan and spat at him in high appreciation. Satan, too, smiled through all the spittle that dripped down his face.

GIRL ON THE ROAD

Veena Nagpal

'STOP IT, AMMA! JUST STOP IT!'

She recoils at my sharp tone, the teaspoon of sweetened yogurt arrested over the bowl in her hand; the words, 'Have a safe journey,' frozen on her tongue.

A twinge of guilt twists my heart but what the hell! She knows I can't afford to be late for today's strategy meet. All the VPs will be there, and the MD too. How can she delay me with all this mumbo jumbo about warding off evil? She's just paranoid—been that way since my only brother died in a road accident. Hurriedly I back out of the gate, ignoring her crestfallen face.

I'm first at the traffic light. Ninety seconds to go.

I grin at my laptop bag. My presentation is good—very good actually. It had better be. I'm aiming to grab that GM-Marketing post.

Sixty-nine seconds...

On my left is a swarm of cyclists and cycle rickshaws, the riders stooped against the cold, mufflers across their noses. One of the cycle rickshaws, with bags and water bottles dangling from hooks on its semi-circular tin roof, is taking chattering children to school.

The light turns green. I step on the accelerator.

Suddenly, a milkman, with huge aluminium canisters on either side of his motorcycle, speeds up from the road to my right, tries to jump the light and almost crashes into me. Crazy guy!

Spoonful of yogurt... her hurt eyes.

I'll make up to Amma in the evening, I promise myself as I head towards the toll road.

Traffic is building up. Now every driver seems angry with everyone else, every vehicle is in a rush. I head towards the Silver Lane. I'm through at last and my speedometer is now reading 100—if only all roads could be like this.

'Idiot!' I scream as an open jeep zig-zags dangerously behind me, passes so close it nicks my left rear-view mirror right out of its bed. Two boys standing in the back of the jeep are guffawing.

'Bhai!' one of them yells. 'Saw that? Girl driving!' He slaps his thigh in merriment.

My blood is boiling. I roll down my left window to yell at them. At the wheel, the driver smiles smugly at the boisterous catcalls of his passengers, turns up the music and zooms away. If I were a Bollywood heroine, I would have raced up, veered sharply in front of the jeep, accosted the driver and made him pay damages...

I'm no heroine. Besides, I can't afford to be late today. I bang my fist on the steering wheel and yell 'Bastard!' inside the closed confines of my car. And then I move on.

Ashram crossing. A virtual ocean of cars, bumper to bumper—nothing moves.

Come on, come on—my foot beats an impatient tattoo. Slight movement now—just a car-length space. I move instinctively. Stop. Inch forward. Stop.

I glance at my watch. Almost ten of the twenty margin minutes I had kept, have been eaten away already. I should have taken the left lane. It seems to be moving faster. My eyes widen—that red jeep again! On my left...

I cast a scorching glance at the driver. Tall, bulky guy wearing a pseudo leather jacket, stubble on his chin. Oh, I know the type—another farmer who has sold ancestral land and with the newly acquired wealth bought a big car he barely knows how to drive. The boys in the rear pass something to him—a hip flask! He takes a swig. They are drinking on the road! In an open jeep in public view! Why is there no policeman to catch this guy? Should I call the police control room?

No, I tell myself sternly. Just get to office. You are not the world's keeper. Besides, you have no time to waste. I take a deep breath, willing my clenched fists to relax. The car behind me honks. The traffic has moved a few feet. I hurry forward to close the gap, stop again...

My mind threatens to return to the red jeep. Sternly I pull it away, chiding myself: What of the mental revision of your presentation you had promised yourself? I groan. Revision? In this cacophony of cars, buses, auto-rickshaws, cyclists, tempos, cows that loiter and squat in the middle of the road, people who cut and obstruct, anyone's brain would become one frothing, unholy mess of fury and frustration. All I want is to get out of this monolithic mass of vehicles crawling painfully like a monstrous reptile inside the city's belly.

Only forty minutes to go and I'm still stuck at the Ashram crossing.

Suddenly the jeep appears again, on my right now, trying to edge its nose ahead of me. He thinks he's very smart. I'm smarter. I move closer to the car in front, closing the tiniest gap. He is on my tail, honking. I can see him in the rear-view mirror. Restless. Crossing lanes—on my right again, parallel. His face is contorted, mouthing angry words. 'You girl! Are you deaf? Can't you hear me honking?'

I lip read his words and I'm like, 'Excuse me! Must I give up my place in the lane just 'cos you are honking?'

That's the way they are, these showoffs of the road—driven solely by their ego and pride.

He manages to edge in. In his rear-view mirror he sees my face twist in anger as I'm forced to give way. He laughs. His companions look delighted. I yell obscenities. He scowls at me, his eyes raging fire.

This is it! At the next police post, I'm going to

complain. What about your presentation, asks my sane inner voice, the post of GM-Marketing? I wince. No, I can't waste precious minutes. I just need to get away. I spot an opening in the left and quickly speed up. Five minutes later, I seem to have lost the red jeep altogether. My pulse eases...

At the crossing, where one road leads into Lajpat Nagar, the market where street vendors peddle rude food and crude crockery, where blue jeans heaped on pavements vie with glass-fronted shops selling wedding finery, and where fat Punjabi women mob Sindhi Sweets for dry fruits and calorie-laden mithai... construction work for the upcoming metro is in full swing, blocking almost the entire road. I concentrate on negotiating the narrow, dusty, potholed passage that has been left for the surging traffic. Suddenly, a vehicle forces me into a pothole. I glance angrily to my left—the jeep!

He has edged in ahead of me and shows me one finger! I ignore the obscenity but suddenly I'm scared.

Spoonful of yogurt to ward off evil—it would have taken me just a split second to swallow it...

In sudden panic, to get away from him, I almost bang an SX 4 on my right. Putting up my hand defensively, I mouth an apology and the silver-haired gentleman in the driver's seat shakes his head and moves on.

I look to my left and right, glance in the rear view mirrors—the jeep seems to have vanished. *Amma must be praying...*

I take a deep breath. In another ten minutes, I should reach my office complex and then I'll be safe.

At the next traffic signal he is there again—on my right! He mouths the word 'bitch'. My face flushes but I restrain myself. Just one more turning and I will be in my own territory. Two minutes later, I see the roadblock right ahead. 'Deep Excavation—Work in Progress', warns the blue Delhi Metro signboard. There's another diversion to the left—pot-holed, dusty.

I glance warily at the rear-view mirror.

'Hit her! Hit the bitch!' the boys are yelling from the back of the jeep. The driver's swarthy face is red with rage. My heart misses a beat. I've never seen such arrogance, so much supercilious scorn, such menace... The corner of his upper lip lifts and sunlight picks the white of his teeth...

I feel like a cornered animal. Suddenly I feel a sense of impending doom. Hurry, hurry, my heart hammers. Right in front of me are the huge, iron signboards. I just have to turn left and...

My neck snaps before I feel the jolt, before I hear the thundering crash... Metal tearing against metal... Tumultuous din. Mayhem... My car is plunging down, the world is falling upon me in clanging, clattering, chaotic clouds of dust. Deep excavation... *Spoonful of... I'm so sorry. I'll make up to you... Amma!*

Screams rip out of me. Breathless.

Crunching sound. My head hits something. I remember

my grandma's nutcracker—the ornate one with a walnut wood handle. Cracking. Loud. Like a million nuts being split at once.

The world spins around me. Sounds fade away...

WHO KILLED MY FAMILY?

Vibha Lohani

MA SITS ON THE FOOTSTEPS OF THE VERANDAH. It is a never-ending wait. She sighs as the sun sets over the horizon. A dried teardrop stains her left cheek. She walks back into the empty house. Yes, it is not a home anymore. Homes echo with laughter. Homes echo with chatter. Homes echo with the sound of children... just the way this house once did. She walks into the kitchen and opens the fridge. Nothing much is stocked in it. Stocking a refrigerator is not required in a house with two lifeless bodies.

She takes out the leftover dough and a bottle gourd. In thirty minutes or less, she conjures up a lifeless meal. She takes a chapatti and some of the vegetable and keeps the rest for Papa. Two years have passed since they had a meal together. Two years... and yet it seems like yesterday.

Papa is at the gate. He doesn't honk the car horn any more. No one runs out to open the gate. He has the keys. Ma is sitting on the sofa watching TV. She continues doing so. Papa walks in, glances at her and walks upstairs to the bedroom. This place seems so different from what I remember. The sound of the television, water running and the pressure cooker are the only sounds that indicate people live in this house. There is no living sound otherwise. Yes, I do hear Ma sobbing sometimes, but that too is muffled by the pillow.

I want to reach out to her. I want to tell Ma and Papa that everything will be alright. But I can't. I am Bunty and I died in a road accident. Two years have gone by... and yet that day is fresh in their memory like it happened yesterday.

◆

Ma stood by the kitchen door, instructing me to do my homework. The TV blared with the sound of a Japanese cartoon dubbed in Hindi. My eyes were glued to the idiot box and while my ears could very well hear Ma's voice, I ignored it. But Ma was always the boss.

'Ma, why did you switch off the television?' I exclaimed.

'You very well know why, Bunty.' Ma gave her standard reply. I knew the tone. She meant business.

'Awww, Ma, just for a little while more.'

'No, complete your work before Papa returns,' said Ma and walked to the kitchen.

'Okay, I will do my homework, but after that you will take me for an ice cream.'

'We will see.'

'And will you let me sit with Papa in the front seat.'

'Bunty, enough, now do your homework.'

Time barely passed and I heard Papa's car reach the gate. He honked twice as usual.

'Ma, Papa is back from office,' I shouted as I ran out of the house. I hopped into the car and sat right beside Papa. 'Ma said we will go for an ice cream. All of us!'

'Did she?'

'Yes, and I will sit with you in the front, Papa.'

Papa smiled. He knew Ma would never allow it, yet he nodded. Just then Ma came out.

'What is taking you both so much time? Pramod, come inside, you must be tired.'

'Jyoti, let's go out for an ice cream,' Papa suggested.

'But Bunty has not completed his homework.'

'Ma, I promise I will do it later.'

Ma shrugged. She locked the house and came to the car.

'Shift to the back seat, Bunty,' she ordered.

'No, I want to sit with Papa.'

'No, Bunty.'

'Okay, then I will sit on Papa's lap.'

'No!' she exclaimed.

'Yes!' Papa and I exclaimed in unison.

'This is not right,' said Ma sternly.

'Nothing will happen, Jyoti. He just pretends to hold the steering wheel while I drive.' Papa seemed to be in a generous mood.

'But, Pramod, he is barely eight years old. Why are you encouraging such things? This can be dangerous.' Ma now sounded upset.

'Jyoti, please relax. Hop onto the driving seat, champ,' said Papa.

'Yippee, I will drive the car,' I squealed and jumped onto Papa's lap. 'Drrrrrrrrrrrrrrrrrrrrrrrrrrrrrrrrr,' I drove along with Papa.

'Smile, Jyoti. See, Bunty is already an expert at driving,' Papa was trying his best to lighten her mood.

'Yes, Ma, see I can drive any car.'

'You are too young to drive a car. You can drive only when you are eighteen,' quipped Ma.

'What rubbish, Jyoti,' remarked Papa, 'I will teach him how to drive by the time he is fourteen.'

'But I already know how to drive, Papa. I have even grown taller. See my feet can reach the brakes.' I wanted to show off.

'Noooo... Bunty, that is the accelerator!' shouted Papa.

Within a split second, the car vaulted into the air. Papa couldn't do anything to control it. We crashed into the pavement and the car overturned.

In just a matter of seconds, I died. My head smashed into the windshield. Shards of glass spread on the road followed by a pool of blood. The ambulance rushed us to the hospital.

'I am sorry, Mr Pramod. Your son is dead,' said the doctor to my Papa who was standing in clothes soaked in blood. Papa started sobbing uncontrollably but Ma seemed too stunned to react. I looked at them. This was unusual. I tried calling out, but my voice did not reach them. Some time later, I am at our home. There is a crowd of people. Their faces are grim. Someone lets out a wail. It is Nani. She has just arrived from Meerut. Her dishevelled look disturbs me. She clings to my body, which is lying on the floor. Ma remains dazed.

Papa isn't crying any more. He just keeps looking at Ma and sometimes at my body.

His eyes are red. Everyone left by and by. Ma and Papa remain. I, too, am here but no one notices.

Two years have passed by. My home doesn't seem like a home anymore. Nothing has been removed from my room. It is cleaned everyday by Ma. I often see her holding my notebook. Tears flow from her eyes but she doesn't speak. Papa moves around mechanically. No one calls out my name anymore. I am just a picture on the wall. Papa feels guilty for letting me sit on the driving seat. He should have known it was dangerous. He feels guilty for not listening to Ma, every time she warned him of the danger.

Ma doesn't blame him. I know she doesn't. She blames herself for not putting her foot down the very first time I sat on the driving seat. She blames herself for not stopping Papa from encouraging me to drive. Both blame themselves for giving into my unreasonable demand. Everyone even remotely connected to my family was hurt that day. An eight-year-old child dying in a family is a catastrophe. No one knew how to console the parents who had lost their child. Time is a great healer they say... but is it really?

People say the accident was not something my parents wanted. How could they foresee what would happen? They should shed off the guilt and move on. But how do dead people move on? Of course it is I who died in that accident; but my entire family was killed that day. And who killed them? Was it me or was it Papa? Or maybe Ma for not stopping us? None of us... My family was killed by the thought—'Nothing will happen.'

ABOUT THE CONTRIBUTORS

About Our Guest Authors

Anand Neelakantan is the bestselling author of *The Rise of Sivagami,* which is book one of the *Baahubali* series, *Asura: Tale of the Vanquished* and the *Ajaya* series. He has written the screenplays for various popular TV series, including the mega series 'Siya Ke Ram', 'Mahabali Hanuman' and 'Chakravarthi Samrat Ashoka', and a script for a soon-to-be-announced Malayalam movie. Having released four titles since 2012, Anand's books have sold over a million copies and have been translated into many regional Indian languages. Anand is considered to be one of the top three fiction writers in India.

Ashwin Sanghi ranks among India's highest selling English fiction authors. He has written several bestsellers—*The Rozabal Line, Chanakya's Chant, The Krishna Key, The Sialkot Saga*—and a *New York Times* bestselling crime thriller *Private India* with James Patterson (and a follow-up titled *Private Delhi*). Included by Forbes India in their Celebrity 100 and winner of the Crossword Popular Choice, Ashwin has also penned non-fiction titles such as *13 Steps to Bloody Good Luck* and *13 Steps to Bloody Good Wealth*.

Kiran Manral is a renowned Indian author, TEDx speaker, columnist, mentor and feminist. She has written books across genres in both fiction and non-fiction. An ex-journalist, her fiction books include *The Reluctant Detective, Once Upon A Crush, All Aboard, The Face at the Window* and *Saving Maya*. Her non-fiction includes *Karmic Kids, A Boy's Guide to Growing Up*, as well as *True Love Stories*. She has had her short stories published in various magazines, anthologies as well as on online apps like Juggernaut. She was part of the core founding team of Child Sexual Abuse Awareness Month and Violence Against Women Awareness Month, two social media initiatives that ran for four years. She also helped initiate India Helps, a volunteer network, which worked on the rehabilitation of 26/11 attack victims.

Pankaj Dubey is a bestselling bi-lingual novelist and filmmaker. Both his books *What A Loser!* and *Ishqiyapa: To Hell With Love* have been written by him in Hindi as well. His writings typically accentuate socio-political undercurrents with wit and humour. He has been a journalist with the BBC World Service in London. He was also selected for the prestigious Writers' Residency in the Seoul Art Space, Yeonhui, Seoul, South Korea amongst three novelists from Asia in 2016.

Priyanka Sinha Jha is a senior journalist and editor who has written widely on Bollywood, celebrities and pop culture in leading publications like *The Indian Express, Screen, Hindustan Times* and *Society Magazine*. She is also the author of a self-help book titled *Supertraits of Superstars*. Having survived a major road accident, she does her bit to increase awareness about road safety.

Shinie Antony is an award-winning writer, editor and columnist. She has written four short story collections, including *The Orphanage for Words* and *Barefoot and Pregnant*, and novels like *When Mira Went Forth and Multiplied* and *A Kingdom For His Love*. She won the Commonwealth Short Story Asia region prize in 2003 for her story *A Dog's Death*. Her latest novel—*The Girl Who Couldn't Love*—will be out this year.

Vikram Kapur is the author of two novels and the editor of an anthology on the 1984 anti-Sikh riots. His short fiction and non-fiction have been published in India and abroad. His short fiction has been shortlisted in several international competitions including, among others, the Commonwealth Short Story Prize. His new novel will be out later this year. He is currently Associate Professor of English at Shiv Nadar University. His website is www.vikramkapur.com

About the Authors of the Stories from the #HASJ Contest

Ambalika is the author of the novel *You Adored, Me Ignored*. When not writing or working as a marketing professional, she likes to go history-poking or practice her skills in the dramatic arts.

Anukriti Verma is a medical intern at Christian Medical College and Hospital, Ludhiana. She lives to travel, meet new people and write about them, not necessarily in that order.

Aritri Chatterjee is a reader, blogger and writer. She aspires to join the publishing industry soon and bring forth fantastic books to readers. Popularly known by the name 'theliquidsunset' on Instagram, Aritri is an active member of the Bookstagram community. You can find out more about her at www.matildareaderofbooks.wordpress.com

Arvind Passey started at the Indian Military Academy and went on to hop jobs from sales to corporate communications to finally settling down to writing. He has published his short stories and poetry in half a dozen anthologies in the UK and India. He writes a column for *The Education Post*, has published articles in *HuffPost, Business Insider, Marketing Buzzar* and other online portals as well. He finally wants to complete his first novel. He blogs at http://passey.info

Barnali Ray Shukla is a filmmaker and a writer. Apart from story and scriptwriting, she writes poetry. She is the India winner of the RaedLeaf Poetry Award 2016. Her book of poems titled *Apostrophe* will be published later this year. Her documentary film 'Liquid Borders' has been doing successful rounds at the film festivals in India, Italy, Canada and USA. She is currently scripting her second feature film, while her first feature film, as a writer-director, 'Kucch Luv Jaisaa' is streaming on Netflix India. She is also shooting her second documentary on the importance of adventure. She lives in Bombay with four hundred books, thirty-nine plants and a husband.

Dipali Taneja grew up in the Delhi of the sixties and seventies, which she can now just about recognise. She is grandmother to three dogs and one young human. Her short stories were published in the Onam Special supplements of *The Times of India*, Kochi, in the nineties. She has been blogging at dipalitaneja.blogspot.in since August 2007. She is the author of *Of This and That*, a collection of short stories, published as a book—a gift from her children on her sixtieth birthday. After living in Thailand, Lucknow, Kochi, Gummidipoondi, and Kolkata, she now lives in Noida.

Geetanjali Maria is a content writer and market researcher who loves to weave thoughts and emotions into short pieces of fiction or poetry. She also wields her pen to voice her opinion on a gamut of socio-political and economic issues.

Ketaki Patwardhan is an anaesthetist by profession and writer by passion. She has written two novels and many short stories, few of which have found a place in paperback anthologies. She loves reading and writing suspense thrillers when she's not busy putting patients to sleep.

Meera Rajagopalan is a writer based in Chennai. Her work has appeared in anthologies in India and the US, and tends to veer around issues of identity. She is currently a freelance writer and a communications consultant for the non-profit sector. Her work has appeared in publications such as *Arts Illustrated, The Times of India* and *Mint Lounge.*

Ratnadip Acharya is a Mumbai-based author. He is the author of two novels—*Life is Always Aimless...* and *Paradise Lost & Regained.* He is a regular contributor to 'The Speaking Tree' in *The Times of India.* He has contributed many write-ups to the *Chicken Soup for the Soul* series.

Anaesthesiologist **Dr Roshan Radhakrishnan** believes in the healing power of love and laughter but practises medicine just to be on the safe side. A winner of Write India Season One, India's largest crowd-sourced literary competition, he has also won the 'Best Blog in India for Creative Writing' for his blog, Godyears.net at the country's first live blogging conference and awards ceremony, WIN'14. Over twenty of his short stories have found their way into anthologies over the years.

Roshni Chhabra is a final year undergraduate at Birla Institute of Technology and Science (BITS) Pilani, pursuing B. Tech in Chemical Engineering. Her hobbies are writing, photography and meeting new people. She loves travelling alone and learning a new art every year.

Sahar Fatima is a software engineer by profession. Her short stories have been published in MuseIndia and induswomanwriting.com. She lives in Bangalore with her husband and two kids.

Sanket Chaudhury enjoys books of diverse genres, and considers reading a vital part of his life. He has a degree in law and a keen interest in writing. He is currently shaping his professional life to become a sports manager.

Taamra Sehgal lives in New Delhi and has been working as a content creator for the last four years. The great-granddaughter of Munshi Premchand, Taamra always wanted to pursue a career in writing. She gave up a career in investment banking in London to pursue her passion in India. Taamra loves gardening, observing people and hopes to write a novel in the near future.

Thommen Jose is a communication consultant based in New Delhi. A travel writer, he has authored two road-tripping books. Wanderink.com is blog.

Veena Nagpal is the author of four novels—*Karmayogi, Compulsion,* and *The Uncommon Memories of Zeenat Qureishi.* Her latest novel *RADIUS 200* was released in April 2017. She has also authored four books for children.

Vibha Lohani is a writer, storyteller, translator and blogger. Many of her stories have been published online as well as offline. She is currently working on a collection of short stories. Being the mother of a seven-year-old, most of her stories are inspired by children. She also conducts storytelling sessions with community children in Noida. She blogs at throughthecolouredglass.wordpress.com